Endorsem.

D0622008

My Dear Kathy,
What a sacred journey you have invited me into by asking me to
read your book! I grew to know you, love you and grieve with
you as I read. It made me wish we could have coffee together
once a week. It caused me to hug my teenagers more tightly and
cling to the Lord knowing that He is faithful through the deepest
of trials. Thank you for influence--asking me to go with you and
Leisha!

I am so sorry for your great loss and your profound grief. Thank
you for surrendering every ounce of it for the glory of God and
the comfort of others. Thank you my friend, my sister.

For the reader:
*Through this beautiful book, Kathy invites you into her naked
heart. You experience her joy, her deepest sorrow and grief
only to witness a resurrection of authentic hope. If you are
walking through trial and grief, God will use this courageous
testimony to breathe new life into you!*

Dr. JULI SLATTERY
President and Co-Founder of Authentic Intimacy
Author of *Surprised by the Healer*
and *25 Questions You're Afraid to Ask*

After the death of her 15- year-old daughter, Leisha, Kathy dares
to enter into the messy places of her pain to give us courage to
look into our own losses. With fierce honesty, she leans into the
darkness to see if God is for real. Inexplicably, Kathy not only
found that God became more real, but that her grief had become
a journey with HOPE! In *Lovely Traces of Hope*, over and over,

Kathy points us to the One who is able to take our brown worlds of grief and transform them into green hope time and time again. This book will restore your faith in God and in his care at the heartbreaking times when we need it most.

VALERIE BELL
President and CEO Awana Clubs International
Speaker, Author of *Well-Tended Soul* and *Faith Shaped Kids*

Is there hope after death? With grace and gut level authenticity, Kathy gently takes you by the hand and leads you to hope that can be found in even the darkest places of your story. I promise you, you will walk away changed after reading Kathy's story!

BECKY HARLING
Popular speaker, author of *The 30 Day Praise Challenge*
and certified life and leadership coach
with The John Maxwell Team

Kathy Burrus lost her daughter, Leisha, in a tragic accident when Leisha was only a teenager. Parents assume their children will outlive them, which makes the loss of a child not only painful but confusing and disorienting. At this point Kathy experienced what literally tens of millions of mothers have experienced throughout human history. But in the wake of the loss she discovered something, which changed everything. She found a journal that contained the beginning of Leisha's life story, a story that was stopped short so suddenly. How many teenagers write their life story? Kathy decided to finish the story. The book you have before you is that finished story.

People's lives carry forward as memory and influence, for good or for ill. This unusual book illustrates such influence in a way that is concrete, moving, and powerful. Normally a daughter carries forward the story of her mother; in this case the mother carries forward the story of the daughter. I am grateful beyond measure that Kathy chose to complete the story. God bless her for it.

JERRY SITTSER, PhD
Professor of theology at Whitworth University
Author of *A Grace Disguised: How the Soul Grows Through Loss*
And *A Grace Revealed: How God Redeems the Story of Your Life*

We've heard it often... 'Sticks and Stones maybe break my bones, but words will never hurt me!'--and we know that's not true. Words can hurt. Conversely, they can reveal things to us that we never knew before and they can heal hurts deeper than we can imagine.

This momma's heart, battered from disappointments, a self-harming child and realizations that she had to let go of a lifelong dream in order to live fully present with her family, was further broken by the tragic loss of her youngest daughter.

But as if whispering from the other side of Heaven ... 15 year old Leisha's own words were a balm to her weary soul.

What do pickles, pinwheels and produce farming have to do with healing and hope? Maybe nothing, maybe everything.

Peek inside these pages to find hearts laid bare ... leaving traces of love, light and ever-present hope.

CARRIE WILKERSON
Speaker and Author of *The Barefoot Executive*

In *Lovely Traces of Hope,* Kathy describes how difficult it can be for us to surrender and to trust our Heavenly Father with every part of our being, to be still and to know that He is God (Psalm 46:10). As I read this book, I was taken back to that time when I had the privilege of walking with Rennie, Kathy, Caitlin, Brielle, and Leisha through some very difficult, gut-wrenching experiences. I watched as Jesus fulfilled his calling to heal the broken hearted (Luke 4:18) and I witnessed a family draw closer to each other as they found that their Heavenly Father was not offended by their questions, or even their doubts.

You will have a better understanding of just how much Abba Father loves you and be able to embrace the truth that hope is on the way when you have taken this journey with Kathy. I highly recommend *Lovely Traces of Hope* and believe healing will result from your having read it.

MARC W. BARNES, Ph.D.
Loveland, Colorado

Lovely Traces of Hope is a poetic and poignant story of the loss of a beloved daughter. Author Kathy instructs and inspires those who choose to move forward in the wake of grief, modeling how to navigate the rocky path from heartbreak to hope and healing.

MARIA GARDNER
Recording Artist and Certified Life Coach

Dearest Kathy,
There are so many words that I would want to write about your love work--yet I will trust that the Spirit has shared with me the words that are most helpful and true for your journey. I love you and admire--beyond words--your courage and tenacity to complete this request from God. I am cheering you on dear friend.

For the reader:
> Hold this story as though you are holding a new life...
> for in many ways you are.

> Read this story of a woman who is learning to trust
> the God of Love through the process of life...
> which for her is through the process of death.

> Behold this story and trust the slow work of God.

BARBARA HUBBELL
Spiritual Director
Lancaster, Ohio

Why is that important to you? How do you see that becoming a part of your life? What would you like your first step to be? How will you feel after you accomplish that? How can I support you right now?

Kathy Burrus is a woman of many questions. Questions she asks from her heart, seeking a way to help others connect with their inner purpose. Her welcoming approach to life is centered around her faith in God and focuses on touching as many lives as she can within her reach. Simply put, Kathy is a servant to positively building the emotional well-being of others.

JENN WENZKE
Life and Business Coach
Founder, *So Now Professional Network for Women*, Northwest Ohio

Life for all of us is a series of joys and sorrows, good times and hard times, new beginnings and loss. In this book you will experience how Kathy has walked through *the Valley of Weeping* and how it has become *a place of refreshing springs, where pools of blessing collect after the rain.* (Psalm 84:6 NLT)

Through her deep grief over many losses in their lives, especially the death of their 15 year old daughter, Leisha, Kathy shares how she met the God of hope, trust and faithfulness in new ways. This book will cause you to reflect on your own life journey and help you search for the God of life, love and hope.

PAT EMERY HIXON, RN, MSN
Retired Director of Nursing

Our greatest gift to others has little to do with our ability, strengths, talents, or successes. Instead it originates in the pain of our deepest wound; in the despair of our darkest night; in the fatigue of our greatest struggle; in the loneliness of our greatest loss. When we are courageous and vulnerable enough to share from those places of our frail humanity, we allow others to embrace their loss, their pain, their struggle . . . and in that moment we shed light on the first step towards healing and hope.

Kathy Burrus offers such a gift to all of us in this beautiful and honest telling of her unwanted journey that began with the loss of her daughter. She does not offer easy answers or religious rhetoric to help manage the pain of loss. Instead, she simply invites us into her struggle, her questions, her anger, her loss, her discovery, her wonder and ultimately her journey towards a present hope. Walk with her and begin to see the green that is everywhere.

RANDY BARGERSTOCK
President, Heart to Honduras
Former Pastor at Crossroads Church of God, Lima, Ohio

In her book, *Lovely Traces of Hope,* Kathy Burrus answers two questions asked by those who ache from deep loss: Will God show up? Is He big enough? Her insights will help those in pain get a new perspective that will bring healing and the courage to move forward. I'm personally blessed by Leisha having included in her journal the acronym God gave me to share with teen girls--B.A.B.E.! I never met Leisha but know she was beautiful, accepted, blessed, and eternally significant. May the lovely traces of her life and love for the Lord live on.

ANDREA STEPHENS
Speaker, Author of *Girlfriend, You Are A B.A.B.E.*
Former Brio Magazine's Beauty Editor, Focus on the Family

Through your incredible story you have captivated my heart and allowed me to walk the painful, difficult but rewarding journey of grief right along-side you. Thank you for taking the risk to be transparent with world and the ones close to you! You have shared with such gut level honesty the ups and downs of grief-- the struggles to hold on and not give up! Praise God you didn't give up. You show each one of us-who take this journey with you as we read your story, how to go through the difficult stuff life hands us. It takes faith to go through--and your faith honored God and God honored your faith. Your testimony is so clear--through *Lovely Traces of Hope* you have come out stronger than you went in, because God was with you all the way! (Isaiah 43:2-3)

BETH BOEHR MILLER
Speaker and Author of Love Legacy
Certified Financial Counselor

Kathy, how very precious your journey is to watch. You, no longer lame, moving and flowing out of Grace. You write differently than before, the broken hard of it all producing a story otherwise unattainable. I can't fathom the pain I know you have walked but I see the beauty unfolding. I thank you for using it to make a difference.

JO ANN FORE
Author of *When a Woman Finds Her Voice*

Lovely Traces of

Hope

By Kathy Burrus
Inspired by Leisha Burrus

www.kathyburrus.com

May you notice the many ways God is showing up in your story and share them with your world with influence, like a dandelion.

Kathy Burrus

Lovely Traces of Hope

By Kathy Burrus

ISBN: 978-0-9978850-3-3

Cover design: Kory Hubbell, HubbellArts (on facebook)
Author Photography: JPMedia Productions, jpmpro.com
Creative Team: Christine Niles, WritersNextStep.com
                Teresa Boyer, ProvisionalPenWriting.com

To My Family

Leisha Danae Burrus

Your life – and even your death- continues to influence a movement of hope! Thank you for the many *lovely traces of hope* you left for me.

I miss you deeply, courageous one.

Caitlin and Brielle

We share this story but not the way we see it or have responded to it. I share so much publicly, you would prefer not to go there. And yet you honor this responsibility I feel to finish Leisha's book--or at least my version of it. Thank you for your trust and your love even when you have felt vulnerable. My heart's cry is that this book will bring added healing and hope -not to the world, but to each of you.

I love you, strength and spirit, to the core.

Rennie

Your support gave me the blessing to sit in my grief from day one when I could do nothing else. Thank you for the endless hours you listened as I processed yet another layer of my ache even as you dealt with your own. I'm so grateful for all the times you supported me, challenged me, taught me, learned from me, held me, wept with me, laughed with me, laid with me, danced with me throughout this entire journey.

I cherish your faithful love, my love.

Our Parents

It is one thing to experience and deal with your own loss, it is quite another to watch your child or your child's child go through it. Thank you for your faithful example of how to walk through each season of life with grace.

To my Mom and Dad (Lovella and Floyd Thiessen):
Thank you for passing on to me a heart for people and a love for words. You continue to model how to love and point others to the Lord. I am most grateful for the long talks as I processed the emotions in these pages.

To Ray and Barbara, my dear parents in love:
Thank you for your lifelong support and encouragement. "Mrs. B", thank you for the writing tools you gave me as my high school English teacher. Thank you for encouraging me to express myself effectively and creatively—then and now

Contents

Foreword by Linda Dillow

What does a mom do when her beautiful, vibrant fifteen year old daughter is suddenly, harshly, instantly gone? Grieve? Of course. Go on a long journey of seeking God and healing? Yes. Kathy did these things but also did something very unusual.

After Leisha died, she opened her daughter's journal and found Leisha's "book." If she flipped Leisha's journal over and upside down and opened the cover, Kathy found her daughter had started to write her own story. She even included the title page.

Lovely Traces

So Kathy began writing to finish Leisha's story.

The Burrus family came to have a vacation in our basement in Colorado Springs in 2002. It was a special time to get to know Kathy, Rennie and their three lovely daughters, Caitlin, Brielle and Leisha. A few short years later, Leisha was singing in heaven and Kathy was finishing her story. As I read *Lovely Traces of Hope*, I smiled, I cried and I wrote these words to Kathy about the book she and Leisha had written.

> *Thank you for walking through the dark tunnel to His Light*
>
> *Thank you for writing so honestly and vulnerably for me and others about grief and pain and how to walk.... believing that there is HIS Light somewhere ahead*
>
> *Thank you for "taking your clothes off" and being real*
>
> *Thank you for revealing the beauty of walking the Christ walk*

Why do I think you should read this book? Let me use Leisha's name to tell you.

L egacy

Both Leisha and Kathy have much to share about building your legacy. Kathy says, *When we intentionally NOTICE what really is happening, it gives us an opportunity to reflect on what we are learning from it. More importantly we see what God has been doing. We NOTICE His fingerprints, HIS HAND on our everyday, ordinary lives. That is especially true when we reckon with the painful areas that may leave us paralyzed in some way. Many times just "noticing" allows us to reframe the events and their effects on our future.*

E ncouragement

As a mom, Kathy gave me hope, showed me how to face problems with teens, how to reach inside myself and be willing to look honestly at "me." We all face loss. Loss is not the defining moment of our lives, it is how we respond to loss that matters. Kathy helped me see in a new way that healing is a progression.

I nfluence

Not many fifteen year olds think about being an influence—they are too busy thinking about boys, clothes or the Friday night party. Leisha wanted to be MAD (Make a Difference)! At her tender age, she thought about being an influence and leaving a legacy. Teens need to read this book!

S incere

Kathy is honest. Listen to her sincere words. *I hesitate to write these next pages. Offering them here is a risk. What will you think of me if I tell of the places in our lives we didn't have it all together? What if I take off the mask enough for you to see me as I really am?*

H oly

Leisha and Kathy's book points you to the Lord God Almighty. In pain. In grief. When life is a dark tunnel, Kathy discovered that God is still Light. She says, *I had to learn to NOTICE God showing up differently.*

A dvance

This book is an advance. It takes you forward in your thinking, in your faith, in your personal journey toward the legacy you are creating. Books have been written on grief. Kathy achingly walks you through how she processed her grief. Books have been written on how to help your teen and whole family walk through trials, Kathy shows you how her family did it.

Leisha and Kathy's combined story is for every mom, every teen....really for everyone. I highly recommend *Lovely Traces of Hope* to you. I promise you it will lead you to hope as it did me!

LINDA DILLOW

Author
Calm My Anxious Heart, Satisfy My Thirsty Soul

Co-Author
Intimate Issues, Passion Pursuit, Surprised by the Healer

Introduction

Journal Entry: August 21, 2006
Lovely Traces of GREEN **HOPE**

The sunlight from my corner kitchen window is streaming in gently as I sit huddled in my chair reading by its light. Tears keep tumbling down my face; one moment from desperate grief, the next in tumultuous gratitude. The book I am reading is not a published work, or ever even read by another person other than its author until now. It is my 15-year-old daughter's journal. A book I had often been curious to peer into, but now I devour it fiercely to know what treasures lay in its pages. My daughter will not be coming in to catch me reading her private thoughts. She will not be returning at all. It has been less than a day since we celebrated her life and said good bye to the precious body that was known by us as Leisha.

The ache in my heart is greater than any I have ever known. I wonder at the pain--at how I can feel it so sharply, yet continue to walk and talk and even laugh out loud at times. It feels that my heart is--not just broken, but rather ripped, violently marred with deep gouging holes that as yet are too shocked to bleed. I so wish it to be a very bad dream. I pray that I will wake up suddenly and realize it is not true.

But I have awakened to see the sun five days now and this nightmare is true.

Still, I sense that the key thing to realize is "I have awakened to see the sun." I slept and it was not a midnight sky I found that first morning after, but a morning sky filled with the promise of a sunrise soon to display its glow.

The night of my child's death, I found sleep.

My first glimpse of the new day had hope of a sunrise. The picture it paints for me even now is one of hope. Hope I have that I shall one day see my sweet daughter again. Hope I have that one day, my husband, my two girls, and I will be able to feel life again, joy again, HOPE again.

For now, I can only hope for hope.

****

It was April 28th, 1991, when our daughter Leisha appeared in our world and messed up all of our plans for the day.

Rennie was the worship pastor and was supposed to be leading a huge dedication service of the new worship center at our church in Pennsylvania. Leisha was being born just as they ended the service with a dedication of the new generation that would grow up in this place. Rennie missed the service. Others had to fill in for him.

She messed up lots of days since then too. Just like every baby does when they grow up in a family! Days become messy and nights interrupted. Plans get changed and that is expected. You know, or at least you realize quickly, when you bring a child into your life they will forever change you.

But Leisha also messed up our lives the day she died.

That was August 16, 2006, yet another mark on all of us that has forced us to look at all of life from a new, yet broken perspective.

Days after Leisha died, we gathered every picture we could find of her and discovered her tapes and journals.

As I opened each journal, I gained access to some of her most personal thoughts of the last few weeks. Many of those had not been private, because she did like to talk. I was glad to see that she had begun a gratitude journal; each evening writing down five things she was thankful for that day.

As I peered through the stories of her life, I found page after page of hope. Struggles turned into victories, hurting relationships of her friends healed or healing through love. Leisha was only 15. Yet I had always known she lived life so urgently--so purposed to go M.A.D (*Make A Difference*), whether it was in the life a friend 'hadn't met yet' or her closest pals--or in me.

It was in her most recent journal that we found 'her book'. If you flipped the journal over and upside down and opened the cover, she had started to write her own story.

She even included the title page.

Lovely Traces

The date she started writing was October 15, 2005 (she was still 14). The next page said "Introduction" and there are 3 blank pages as if she was to come back to fill them, or perhaps she left them for me to finish.

Then...

Chapter One   *Once Upon A Time...*   *By Leisha D. Burrus*

How many stories do you know that begin with 'once upon a time"? Well this is one of them, or so I thought. I was born April twenty-eighth, nineteen ninety one. But wait! I am getting ahead of myself. I guess I should start where it all began.

My parents met in high school. ... and she begins to tell the love story of her dad & me.

As I sat there reading it for the first time, I could imagine this book was to be full of adventure and relationships and truth. Such truth! Because even in the short chapter that was written, she had spoken much truth to my heart. I knew the stories of her life; I had lived them with her. But now I was looking at them from an opposing vantage point. Events I knew to have meaning as they happened, suddenly took on vivid clarity. The fact that she chose these specific things to share in her chapter told me of their significance to her.

Just as Leisha had penned these few words to begin writing her story, she died. Not only was her life unlived, but her story unwritten.

I knew the moment I read her words "I should start where it all began" when she began telling my story that it was meant for me to finish. Her story started with mine. It was as if she knew I would need a jump start.

Earlier that morning I had picked up my Bible to continue reading where I had left off the day before. I read these words from Revelation 1:

> [17] **When I saw him,** *I fell at his feet as if I were dead. But he laid his right hand on me and said, "Don't be afraid! I am the First and the Last.* [18] *I am the* **living one. I died, but look—I am alive forever and ever!** *And I hold the keys of death and the grave.*
>
> [19] *"***Write down what you have seen—both the things that are now happening and the things that will happen.**[1]

The words in bold jumped off the page at me.

Living One Who Died! I had not heard Jesus described that way before. Don't get me wrong! I grew up in the church. I had heard about Jesus every Sunday. I celebrated many a Christmas and Easter replaying the story of Jesus being born to a virgin. I knew he lived, then died and yet rose again! I could quote you scriptures that spoke of him being the resurrection and the life.

But now I see this same Jesus--this **Living One who Died**--holding the keys to the place of death, to the place Leisha's body has been laid.

I felt Leisha writing these words to me.

> *"Mom! When I saw the Living One who died, I fell at his feet...and he put his hand on me and said "don't be afraid. I'm not, mom! Don't you be afraid either. Mom, you've got to write! Now! Write down what you have seen--what's happening right now and all the things that are going to happen. You can do it Mom!"*

So I write ... to finish a story!

I'm writing to finish the story Leisha started.
I'm writing to tell my own story.

But it is my hope that this is not just another book you read, and maybe share with a friend or slide on to yet another full shelf of stories. It is my hope that my story and the journey it takes you on allows you to experience transformation too. With everything in me I pray that it will point you to hope.

After Leisha died, I ferociously devoured stories that others wrote, not because I needed to hear yet another story that included pain or loss, or even that I wanted to see how people overcame those tremendous hurts. No, I read because I had to find out two things:

- Did God show up in their story?

- Was he big enough for the pain?

My primary goal in writing is to share with you about the many ways this **Living One who Died** showed up in our story. Yes he did! He showed up! Different than we expected him to be, but he was there, over and over again.

That's the real story in my life and yours!

As to whether he is big enough, well, you will just have to read the book to find out.

LET'S START AT THE BEGINNING

1 Leisha's Chapter 1

Once Upon A Time...   By Leisha D. Burrus

How many stories do you know that begin with "once upon a time"? Well this is one of them, or so I thought. I was born April twenty-eighth, nineteen ninety one. But wait! I am getting ahead of myself. I guess I should start where it all began.

My parents met in high school. Well, actually, my mom knew who my dad was for a long time before that, but they started to date in high school. They went to the same college and eventually got married. They had both been raised in Texas, so it was natural that their first child (my oldest sister, Caitlin) would be born in Texas. Dad was in seminary at the time and shortly after Caitlin was born, he had a chance to work at a church in Pennsylvania called Calvary. At that time, they lived in a medium sized yellow house (sound like a fairy tale yet?) where my second oldest sister, Brielle, was born.

So there they are, happy little family in a yellow house while the man of the house is off being a great assistant pastor and his two perfect pastor's daughters and his perfect pastor's wife are home playing and growing and having a grand old time being perfect (or trying anyway).

Then a good friend of mom's had a miscarriage of her third child. At that point, Mom and Dad had decided to wait to have more children, but by then it was too late. I was on my way. My mom was devastated at the thought of a third child right now when her good friend had just lost her third. My mother could not believe God had let her have this baby inside of her. She couldn't handle it. She did not want and could not handle another child right now. But then one morning when she woke up she saw... *(Leisha left a blank, I'm sure she was going to ask me to tell her again what I had seen. It was a calendar picture of a kangaroo with a baby roo inside her pouch. The caption read, "Do not neglect the gift that is in you!")* Then she knew that God was going to use this baby and even as hard as it was for her to accept it, she did. And I was born.

Daddy was the children's pastor (*actually Worship Pastor and Single Adults, but sometimes they seemed like big kids!*) at Calvary at the time. It was a dedication Sunday. If you don't know what a dedication Sunday is, it is a Sunday that parents dedicate their babies to the church and to God. Dad was the one in charge of it. Except he was with his wife at the hospital having one of their own! ME!

So April 28th, 1991, on a Sunday afternoon in Honeybrook, Pennsylvania at Brandywine Hospital, they had a little baby girl named Leisha Danae Burrus.

Now my once upon a time begins!

2 Where Did it Begin?

I really wasn't all that surprised that Leisha interrupted the story she was telling about her life to "start at the beginning". We had often talked about the fact that we are all part of a bigger story; one that includes a lot of people who have lived before us. So Leisha went back to my story; a day when 'boy met girl' and fell in love, married and had children.

She started her story with mine. I could tell my story and go back to the love story of my parents, and my mother could do the same as could my grandmother and her mother before her if they were still on earth. We had often talked about those people who came before us. My mom had spent years researching the genealogy of my family. On some family lines, mom was able to trace our family history back about 14 generations.

It is much like reading those "begat" chapters in the Bible such as Matthew 1. By the way, I looked up the definition of 'begat'. It means "*to produce or bring forth*" or more specifically "*produce offspring.*" In Matthew, it specifically means that one man fathered the next son, who fathered the next, and so on.

Because of the wealth of information we have from my mom's study, I can create a "begat" list too. Most often in the Bible, they share the father's name, though some women are mentioned in the different family lines. Since this is Leisha's story, and I am writing this as her mom, I'm going to use my mother's side of our genealogy. So my 'begat' chapter from my mother's side might look something like this.

...(<u>I don't know this person's name</u>) but she begat Helena Spence Eitzen

     Helena begat Helena Eitzen Kornelson

     Helena begat Katherine Toews Schierling

     Katherine begat Elizabeth Schierling Thiessen

     Elizabeth begat Lovella Thiessen Thiessen

     (Yes, her maiden name was the same last name as my father's, though they have gone back 14 generations and not found they were related)

     Lovella begat Kathlyn Thiessen Burrus

     And Kathlyn (and Rennie) begat Leisha Danae Burrus, born April 28, 1991 in Brandywine Hospital, in Coatesville, Pennsylvania.

You get the idea!

As I went through Mom's book on our genealogy, I was struck by the fact that I only knew two of these women before me; my mother and my grandmother. Leisha only knew me and my mom. Though we do have a picture of her being held by my grandmother before she died, I don't think Leisha was old enough to remember her.

I remember hearing stories about my great grandmother. One special story I remember is that on her death bed, Great Grandmother Katherine could tell my grandmother was pregnant with my mom just by holding her hand, even before Grandma had told her.

My grandmother lived several hours away from us, so we saw her only a couple of times a year. But I remember feeding the chickens and taking lunch out to Grandpa and the uncles at harvest time. And there were countless times at her kitchen table making pinwheel cookies rolled in 3 colors of dough; pink, brown and plain. They were a favorite of all the grandchildren.

Lovely Traces of Hope

She also taught me to love a great dill pickle. I remember the day as a 7 or 8-year-old we went down to her cellar and brought up some of her precious canned goods for our evening meal. Among them was a jar of pickles. She pretended to sneak it to the counter to open it without anyone but me knowing because she knew I liked pickles. She pulled out a whole pickle with a fork and motioned for me to take it. "I think we will keep these to ourselves, is that ok?" We winked at each other all through dinner because we kept that pickle plate down by us. I think we ate the whole jar that day. That was always our special memory.

Why do I share silly stories of pinwheel cookies and pickles with you? Because my grandmother doing ordinary things touched my life in extraordinary ways! The day she died, I literally felt the loss of her presence in my life. She had been a strong and faithful prayer warrior since before I was born. The worth of her legacy is priceless.

I am left with stories of these women that have laid the groundwork for the life Leisha --and I--were born into. Yet, I didn't even know some of their names before Mom looked them up. I wondered if the lives they lived and the decisions they made still have an impact on me today.

My mom, Leisha's grandmother, created a book of genealogy for each grandchild when they were born. At the beginning of the book, Mom wrote these words.

Dear Leisha
To you has been given a heritage. You did not earn it or even ask for it. It is just yours. Like it or not, these people who have lived before you have given you something. From them have come some of your characteristics. People will say you even look like them, or talk or act, or even react like some of them.

Here in these pages lie nothing about your future, except what you learn from your past. If it has been good, use it to build upon. From the mistakes you find out about your ancestors, learn too. By God's grace they need not be repeated.

As you celebrate your 1st Christmas, you will be told how God, the Heavenly Father gave His Only Son. That is a story even more important for it is the REAL HERITAGE.

Psalm 44:1 We have heard with our ears, O God, our fathers have told us, what work thou didst in their days, in the times of old. [2]

Psalm 78:4 We will not hide them from their children, showing to the generation to come the praises of the Lord, and his strength, and His wonderful works that He hath done. [3]

Grandma Thiessen [1]

While I'll never know how much Leisha understood about her history, she did acknowledge that her story did not begin the day she was born. Do you remember the line from Tolkien's *Lord of the Rings* when Sam, the Hobbit gardener turned body guard speaks to Frodo, the unsuspecting Hobbit hero? They were recovering from a horrific battle in their attempt to save the world. Sam looks out over the remnants of the battle field while Frodo rests, burdened by the weight of it all.

Sam muses, "I wonder what sort of tale we've fallen into?" [4]

What a great question for all of us to ask of our own stories!

Our world didn't start with us! Just like Sam, Leisha accepted that there was something larger going on than just her story or mine. Think about that! When you were born, there was a story already being written by your parents and people you probably never heard of.

We all 'fell into' a tale that was introducing us into the world. If we trace it back far enough, our story is a continuation of an even bigger story of all time; the God story that is recorded in the Bible. So this is not Leisha's story, or my story, but our story. I continue to be amazed at how God has shown up. I believe he is very much a part of yours as well.

But the problem is, somewhere in the routine of life, and the mundane chores, and kid's activities and our job, we've forgotten life is about much more. We've come to accept that events in our days are random happenings rather than God designed opportunities to experience life as God intended. We fail to see him break into our world and speak his love and grace in an unlovely place.

I'm reminded that another definition of the word 'begat' is *to cause, to produce as an effect.* If you and I become intentional about understanding our stories and the chapters we have yet to write, we can 'beget', or cause, some influence into the lives we touch, just as the generations before Leisha have spoken into her story.

Writing this book from the perspective of the death of my daughter changes how I view some of the stories on these pages. Leisha had no warning that her life was over. She would not have chosen to die that day. But as I viewed the writings in her journal, I saw (and heard) her say what she wanted to be true of her in life. I noticed how her desire had influenced some of the decisions she had made even as a teenager.

She started with the end in mind. Wow! That was not a new concept from her. It is an age old principle, but one she grabbed up even at the young age of 15.

When she died, Leisha was just beginning to understand what kind of effect she wanted to have. Another word for that is *influence.* Just minutes before she died I was teasing her about her impatience to turn 15 ½ and get her driver's permit. I jokingly said, "You just want power!" She paused, but I could see the wheels turning in her head.

Then she thoughtfully said words I'll never forget! "Mom, I don't want power. I want to influence. I want to be able to say, I'm going--come with me!"

I stroked her nose like I had many days since she was born and affirmed, "Honey, you were made to influence." Ten minutes later, she died.

But her influence did not. She continues to *beget* influence in my life, her sisters, her family and friends. People that never even knew her have spoken to us of the *influence* her death had on them personally.

Leisha did life on purpose. Though we redecorated her room for her 4th anniversary, there is a computer generated page that remains where she placed it on the back of her bedroom door. It contains her *intentionals;* her list of life values that gave her perspective for the life she wanted to live. It reads:

I will not judge people by their appearance.

I will keep myself pure for my future husband.

I will work hard to learn more about God and become closer to him.

I will try to look at things from a positive standpoint.

I will try to be humble and keep a Christ-like attitude in all that I do.

I will encourage and not put down others.

I will try to obey all authority figures.

I will maintain a strong self-image and confidence.

I will learn from my mistakes, and when I fall I will pray for guidance.

My name is Leisha Danae Burrus
And I am a Christian.

It breaks my heart that she won't be included on a *'begat'* list anymore. Her line is done in that regard. But her choices, her *'intentional'* list and the way she lived it out will continue to influence those closest to her, even *"friends she hadn't met yet"* as Leisha would call most strangers.

That's her legacy! I'm writing this in a mom's effort to continue her influence.

But I am still here. What is my legacy? Any previous vision I had for the end of my life did not include one of my daughter's preceding me in death. Any plans I was making for my life were completely shattered the day she died.

I can choose to be consumed by her death and the ache I still feel every day. Or I can re-start with the end in mind. I still have an opportunity to build on my own legacy; to create a new list of *intentionals* for what I want to be true of myself.

As a wife, a mom, daughter, friend, I intentionally seek to love in a way my family will feel love. No, I'm not perfect at it, but I want more than anything for each family member to know I love and accept them for who they are--not for who I want them to be.

As a life and marriage coach and speaker, I work with women and couples to *intentionally design hope as they engage life, empower love and embrace loss*. I long to help others accept their entire story as they learn from their past and move toward their future. It's not just what I do for a living, but what I do because of who I am. It's what I do no matter what role I'm in-- wife, mom, coach or pastor's wife. It is part of the dream and design God gave me many years ago.

As a worship leader, I intentionally choose to be a worshiper first. To sit at the feet of my Savior, to know his face, to recognize his voice and then lead others to him.

Through Leisha's invitation to finish this book, I am now a writer. But I write not just to be a writer, but rather to be influencer and a pointer in many ways;
- a pointer to hope,
- a pointer to life,
- a pointer to **The Living One who died and shows up** in our stories every day, even if we don't notice.

Leisha influenced me to see him even after she died. Now I point you to him. If you, dear reader, are able to intentionally notice him in your own story and then help others see him in their story, then you are part of that legacy too.

3 Boy Meets Girl

Leisha's version:
My parents met in high school. Well, actually, my mom knew who my dad was for a long time before that but they started to date in high school. They went to the same college and eventually got married. - Leisha Burrus

My version:

I had known Rennie a long time before high school. He went to another small town elementary school in the Texas panhandle. We both took part in the local 4-H chapters in our towns. When I was 9-years-old, I attended a county wide 4-H banquet presided over by an 11-year-old boy who seemed to have abundant confidence. His name was Rennie Burrus. I remember thinking how courageous he was to be able to do that at such a young age. And he was cute too!

Rennie and his brother, Devin, changed schools when his mom, Barbara Burrus, otherwise known as "Mrs. B", came to teach high school English at my school. Rennie was an 8th grader, while Devin and I were in the 7th grade. I don't think Rennie noticed me at all until perhaps my sophomore year.

At the end of that school year in 1974 when I was almost 16, Mrs. Buckner, the mother of the reigning Miss Lipscomb County came to me with an offer to be part of the county's local beauty pageant over the 4th of July weekend. She had spoken with almost every teen girl in the county. I giggled at her suggestion and graciously listened as she gave me all the details, but quickly gave her back the forms and declined the offer.

She was very encouraging and once again began to tell me all the benefits of such an event. I could see that it would be a great opportunity and I was certain it would be great fun. I had grown up watching other Miss America or Miss USA pageants, and had often dreamed of being the one on whom they placed the crown, but once again I said, 'no thank you!"

 This determined chairwoman of the beauty pageant committee was of the persistent sort.   She finally said to me a bit exasperated, "Kathy, why not?" I said, "I'm not good enough." Actually that's not what I said. I used words like, "I'm a preacher's kid and preacher's kids can't do that kind of stuff." But as I looked back, I realized I was saying, "I'm not good enough."

I had barely walked in the front door after school that afternoon when my parents called me into the kitchen. It seemed that my conversation with the Pageant chairwoman had already made its way to their ears. I chuckled. My goodness, Mrs. Buckner doesn't give up easily!

My parents asked me about the pageant, what I knew of it, and whether I would like to be in it. I told them what I knew, and said, "Sure, it would be fun! But I understand that I can't do it, so I'm good with it."

Then my dad said something I never expected!

"We have two weeks until you need to decide. Let's take that time to pray about it and see what God would want you to do."

I was a bit surprised, but, duh! Of course you have to pray about it first. That way when God says no, you have a good reason to tell the chairwoman no. So I agreed to pray about it.

But truly, I don't think I ever thought about it again. Why pray? I already knew the answer would be no.

Two weeks later, my parents come to me again. We had not spoken of the pageant or praying about it since that first conversation. I was once again surprised that they brought it up.

"So what do you think God wants you to do about the pageant?" Dad asked. I gulped! Dad wasn't often the one to ask those questions. I usually had these discussions with mom. "Well," I stammered! "I understand that as a preacher's kid (notice I'm still blaming it on being a preacher's kid), I need to live a life that's pleasing to God, so I understand that I can't do it."

"Really?" Dad questioned. "Well, your mother and I think that you should. We feel God opening doors for you here! We think you should fill out the papers and get going."

I'm not sure what I looked like at that moment. My chin must have dropped to the floor and my eyes bugged out. My parents smiled at each other. You didn't have to tell me twice. If God said yes, and my parents heard it, it must be important. I immediately regretted that I had given back the forms that day of my initial conversation with the chairwoman. Just as quickly, my mom handed me everything I needed to get registered.

That was the day my parents AND that pesky Mrs. Buckner became my heroes. They saw beyond the idea of the beauty pageant to the heart of a young girl. A girl that was hiding behind the mask of being a preacher's kid instead of being honest and saying I don't feel "good enough" to take that giant step. Their belief in me was the beginning of learning to believe in myself and in the intimate involvement of the God who created me.

That insight in itself was a life changing moment for me! God showed up in my story! I had seen him!

I entered that pageant and had the time of my life. I not only got to learn to model, and shop for the right dress and shoes and meet some of the most interesting local leaders, but I got to hang out with girls from all over the county, several of whom became heroes in time. I was relaxed. I felt confident. I thoroughly enjoyed every minute of it.

The day of the pageant included interviews with the judges. One of them, Helene Jayroe, was the mother of Jane Anne Jayroe, Miss Oklahoma 1966 and Miss America 1967. I was thrilled to be able to meet the mom of a woman I had so admired as a young girl, but found myself just as taken with Helene as we spoke.

After a beautiful luncheon with the judges, we all hurried to the dressing rooms to get ready for the big event. We modeled sportswear first, then it was evening gowns.

I remember standing near the back of the stage, peeking from behind the curtains, just drinking it all in. One by one, each girl made her way around the platform. When it was my turn, I just felt like I was floating. Here I was modeling before the entire county, a beautiful light pink gown my mom had sewn for just this occasion. And I didn't even trip in my tall, silver heels. What fun! I couldn't stop smiling!

The moment came for the announcement of the top 5 finalists. I was pretty sure who all would make it. There were 3 girls who were certain to get in. One of them even had her hair teased and was ready for the crown to be placed there. There were a couple of others who seemed to know just what to do and say. I was pretty sure they would complete the group. They were 'popular' enough.

Sure enough, they called the girl with the hairdo and the other two. I wasn't at all surprised. But the next one, well, I was pleased. She wasn't all that popular. I was glad that the judges had been able to see all the neat things about her. Even in the middle of all my thoughts, I suddenly became aware that they had called the last name.

Slowly it dawned on me that it was my name. Kathy Thiessen! That was me! They called my name!

I felt frozen in place. The girl next to me reached over to give me a push forward. I had not even dared to think this might be a possibility, let alone bothered to prepare for the question they would ask the finalists at the end. I never dreamed I would get to this point. Yet here I stood, waiting for the question that could decide my fate. I didn't care. How fun to be here right now! How amazing to not only be allowed the opportunity to be in the pageant, but to be honored to be part of the top five finalists.

My heart soared!

Soon I was being addressed by the Master of Ceremonies. His question was pretty simple. "If you could be anyone living in the world today, who would you be?"

I quickly thought through a long list of people that I could probably say:

- The President? No way, though maybe the president's wife.
- A favorite actress or musician? No, I admired many, but I really didn't want to be them.

- An author? All the authors I could think of at the time were dead.

I know there were a lot more ideas, but it seemed like I had used too much time thinking already.

So...I said what every girl at the age of 16 says when asked this question, (well, at least this 16-year-old.)

"My Mom!"

I gave a lot of reasons to appreciate and admire my mom, top of which was her patience in putting up with me getting ready for this event. But I shook my head and as I walked back to my place, I mumbled to myself, "Can't imagine that's going to win me any crown!"

Then the moment came! I didn't care that I would be the first name called as 4th runner up. I went from feeling like I was not good enough to being a finalist. That meant a lot to me.

But they called the name of the 4th runner up and it wasn't me. I was a bit dazed.

They called the 3rd and 2nd runners up and again, it wasn't me.

Suddenly it occurred to me that I was standing next to the girl with the hairdo, holding hands, scarcely able to breathe.

"And the first runner up is..."and it wasn't me!

I was shocked! So was the girl with the hair! How could it be? Lord!

What does this mean? I'm a 'nobody'! How is it that an ordinary girl, a preacher's daughter to boot, could win an event that by its very nature said "You're Special"? I wanted to be special. I had often prayed, even as a very young girl, that one day God would make me special. But never in my wildest dreams did I imagine that I would feel that way as MISS LIPSCOMB COUNTY 1974.

Why did I tell you this story? Was it so you would know that I'm somebody important? No! To most of the world, this was no big deal.

For me, it was a God moment. I can, even after all these years, recite back to you every minute detail of that event--not just the pageant, but of details that brought me to that moment.

That's because God broke into my world. He connected with one of the few dreams I had ever spoken outright--to be a Miss Somebody. I know it is not Miss America, but at 16 it felt like it. The irony is that I never dreamed that dream could happen. I was not doing anything to pursue it. I wasn't working to make it happen.

I saw God take all the loose ends of my young life and tie them together in that event. ***He showed up in a way I would notice.***

I NOTICED what changed for me:

- That God was not only identifying a false message I had believed since I was young, but he was replacing it with the truth that he had made me special. Does that mean all the other girls were not? Absolutely not! But at that moment in my story, he chose to use this to speak to me.

- That God wants me to seek him in prayer because he is intimately involved in my life and desires to be known by me. He wants me to see that he sees me.

- That God places people in our lives, like my parents and the pageant chairwoman, to speak into our lives. People that can see something we cannot. People that believe in us and challenge us to new heights.

- That part of my God-given design, and part of a new dream that was beginning to form in me was to be an up-front person. A person who is able to lead from a stage, maybe on a worship team, maybe as a speaker, or a coach. But in each instance using my influence to speak into the lives of others. There have been many times since then that I have reflected back on that moment to gain courage to take my next bold step.

What does this have to do with Leisha's story? Well, aside from the amazing lessons I carried with me the rest of my life, that wasn't all that was special about that night.

You see after the pageant was over, the curtain had closed and the hugs from the girls who had been with me on stage began to subside, two young men from my school appeared from back stage. Both gave me a hug. But as I looked over the shoulder of the tallest one, I got a wink from the other. It wasn't for winning the contest, but for winning the attention of the young man holding me.

Yes, his name was Rennie Burrus. It wasn't long after that we started dating.

One of my favorite memories was of our third date. I actually can't remember what we did that night. But when he brought me home we sat in the driveway talking.

I asked him what he wanted to do when he grew up. He hesitated. "You will laugh if I tell you."

I was almost offended. I work very hard not to hurt people's feelings. I promised him I would not laugh; I truly was interested.

"I've always thought about being a pastor!"

I choked back a laugh, surprising even myself.

"I told you that you would laugh."

"No, I'm sorry. I'm not laughing at you. It's just that..." Then I hesitated. "It's just that I've always dreamed I'd be a pastor's wife."

Funny thing! He didn't laugh. Hmmmm?

Five years later, nearing the end of college as we were preparing for ministry, we were married. June 9, 1979.

AND THEN I WAS BORN

4 Do Not Neglect the Gift in You!

Leisha's version:

They had both been raised in Texas, so it was natural that their first child (my oldest sister, Caitlin) would be born in Texas. Dad was in seminary at the time and shortly after Caitlin was born, he had a chance to work at a church in Pennsylvania called Calvary. At that time, they lived in a medium sized yellow house (sound like a fairy tale yet?) where my second oldest sister, Brielle, was born.

Then a good friend of mom had a miscarriage of her third child. By that point, Mom and Dad had decided to wait to have more children, but by then it was too late. I was on my way. My mom was devastated at the thought of a third child right now when her good friend had just lost her third. My mother could not believe God had let her have this baby inside of her. She couldn't handle it. She did not want and could not handle another child right now. But then one morning when she woke up she saw... (Leisha left a blank, I'm sure she was going to ask me to tell her again what I had seen. It was a calendar picture of a kangaroo with a baby roo inside her pouch. The caption read, "Do not neglect the gift that is in you!") Then she knew that God was going to use this baby and even as hard as it was for her to accept it, she did. And I was born. - Leisha Burrus

My version:

They say that hindsight is 20/20 vision. I've come to believe that is not always true! We can experience our life and yet never really know what it is teaching us.

You have probably heard that the reason the windshield is so large in the front of our car and the rear view mirror is so small is because what's happened in your past is not nearly as important as what's in your future.

Ok! There is much truth there. It is important that we get a clear perspective of what is ahead and where we are going. With that in mind we can increase the momentum to reaching our destination. If we spend so much time focusing on our past, we can literally come to a complete halt with any forward movement.

But we have a rear view mirror for a reason! We need to at least give it appropriate consideration.

Too often we blitz through life, and through circumstances and relationships always looking at the next thing in the windshield and never checking the rear view mirror. I'm not talking just 20 or 30 years back. I'm talking about what happened this morning in the conversation with our spouse, or the issue that came up at work last week.

Whether we are seeing clearly or not depends on our willingness to look back and intentionally reflect on how significant events or relationships impact our story. That is the real gift of the story.

I've used a tool to help me get some perspective on my life called a Life Map! The Life Map allows me to consider the impact of the 4-H's of my story: (Burrus, *What's Your Story Telling You? Pg 31)[1]*

- HERITAGE: those things that are part of my life strictly because of to whom, when and where I was born. It is the stuff about you that is so ordinary you probably don't even realize how it continues to influence you.
- HIGH POINTS: transformational or pivotal points in my life which are good and fulfilling.
- HARD TIMES: transformational or pivotal points in my life which are harmful or negating.
- HEROES (or un-heroes/villains): significant people that have impacted my life for good (or bad).[2]

If I asked you to tell me a significant part of your story, chances are you would pick something related to the hard times or the un-heroes of your story. I don't know why we do that, but that is usually where we keep our focus.

But what if we pulled back from our story to take a look at the big picture? What if we put those hard times in perspective with the high points and heroes of our story? Is there a chance (and I believe there is) that we would see more clearly how those hard times have played into the high points?

As a life coach, I primarily help people look forward. We create our vision for the future and ask questions like 'where do you want to go?' or 'What will it take to get there?'

However, often as we try to take forward steps we realize we have this chain on our ankle that keeps us anchored to the past. This is usually because the past circumstance or relationship has taught us to believe something which continues to create links in that chain. Unless we take some time to look back and identify the messages of the past, we often cannot break its hold on us and move forward.

Simply *remembering* the past is not enough. That would be like watching a movie over and over and never identifying the main idea of the movie.

But when we intentionally (yes, there is that word again) NOTICE what really is happening, it gives us an opportunity to reflect on what we are learning from it. More importantly we see what God has been doing. We NOTICE His fingerprints, HIS HAND (which is now a 5th H) on our everyday, ordinary lives. That is especially true when we reckon with the painful areas that may leave us paralyzed in some way. Many times just "noticing" allows us to reframe the events and their effects on our future!

If I were to show you my Life Map, I could tell you of many transformational events and influential people in my life. One very significant event in my life also began with someone else's story. Leisha wrote what she knew of it in her chapter. I felt it was important for me to share it with her. I wanted her to know how God had showed up in my story to remind me of the gift she was to us.

Rennie and I were living in Pennsylvania. Ren was pastoring at Calvary Fellowship Church. Our two oldest daughters had already been born, Caitlin in Texas and Brielle after we moved to Pennsylvania.

A friend, Maureen, announced she was pregnant. That was great news! They had experienced many miscarriages and difficult pregnancies, one resulting in a still born baby boy. Another pregnancy was twins; however, the baby boy died in utero. The little girl survived and was born full term, healthy and beautiful.

Now Maureen was pregnant again and everything was going great. We were thrilled it was a boy. Maureen shared with me that she had been in the hospital with placenta Previa for 5 weeks prior to his delivery. Everything was going well until she had a small amount of bleeding and that's when everything began to unravel. The nurse failed to balance the scale and so she reported that the bleeding was heavier than it actually was. Her doctor ordered an amnio to check to see if Eric's lungs were developed so he could be delivered before Labor Day weekend and the amnio wasn't done properly.

In the days that followed, the doctors said there were several chances to save him, but "everything kept going wrong, and he just was not meant to be". Little Eric was born just days from being strong enough to breathe on his own. For the next month he fought to live.

It was just after his birth that I found out I was pregnant with our third child. I was completely overwhelmed. I was unsure if I was ready for another child and my friend was fighting desperately for hers. Somewhere in the middle of all these emotions, I came up with this brilliant plan. I knew God would see the wisdom.

"If a baby has to die--take mine! Maureen has survived many miscarriages, I'm sure I can also, even though it will be hard. Let her have her baby!"

But a month later, baby Eric died. My baby continued to grow.

For the next four months, I fought with God! How could you let this happen? I gave you an out! I offered you my child. Don't you know she NEEDED that baby to live?

How can I trust you anymore?

Then it hit me! I was yelling at God...for being God! It was a shock to my theology that something could happen that I didn't like- and God could still be good, still be right and still be in control.

It struck me that once again God was doing something "outside of the box" I had made for him. You know the one. It's where we place all the parts and pieces of our lives, including God, and everything else all fits neatly inside. And we are happy!

When he does something radical and blows the lid off our box or busts out the sides, we have two choices. We can be angry and bitter, and dismiss God as being weak-willed and capable of making mistakes as I did; OR we can allow God to expand the box to encompass all that happened as being from him.

It was late New Year's Eve 1990. Ren was gone to an Urbana mission's conference with a group of our Single Adults. I lay back in my bed, so weary of the incessant battle going on in my heart. I sobbed, "O God, I choose to trust YOU!" I trust you with Maureen's story, with mine, and with my baby's!

The next morning as I rolled over in bed, I noticed the calendar on my wall. I had not changed the pages since August when Baby Eric died. It was now December. It had been there a long time, but for the first time I saw the calendar picture of a kangaroo with a baby roo inside her pouch. The caption read, "Do not neglect the gift that is in you!" The verse was 1 Timothy 4:14. (A passage that later came to be special to Leisha.)

Four months later, Leisha was born beautiful, healthy, and already doing things her own way.

It was when I reflected on this story that I saw God:

- I saw God show up because I stopped to notice what had really happened in this part of my story.

- I saw God show up because I dared to yell at him for allowing something I didn't like, but he didn't yell back. This message came back to me after Leisha died.

- I saw that God didn't force me to trust him. It was a choice I had to make.

- I saw God show up in Maureen! She wrote to me recently. She recalled those well-meaning friends and even medical staff who would come into her room and say to her, "This baby was just not meant to be." Her response then and now was, "*I know Eric was meant to be, even if he only had an impact on my life.*" I reassured her that her baby boy and my wrestling match with God is a huge part of my story which I share often. Eric continues to influence lives just as Maureen has influenced mine.

- I saw God show up on a calendar of all things. Ok! There was scripture on the calendar, but he had my attention.

Sometimes because God's presence or his behavior isn't what we think it will be, we don't pay attention and we miss him. But when we stop and reflect on the current and past events in our lives, or the relationships that are tied to those events, we begin to see a thread of the message we were meant to see. Those messages were directly tied to how I saw God show up for me.

There have been many times in my life that I have reflected back to those moments when I wrestled with God. And he let me! He didn't yell back at me, but let me pound on his chest until I couldn't pound anymore. Then in a still quiet voice with words from a calendar, he spoke. Take care of your baby! Don't neglect the gift I have given you!

I have seen even in the process of writing this book that 'the gift' is not just my child. It is also all that I have learned from this story as it pointed me to my future.

Author Dan Allender writes, *God is constantly writing our story, but he doesn't send us the next chapter to read in advance. Instead, we all read backward, finding the meaning in our stories as we read what God has already written."* [3] *(pg 10)*

No, we can't drive a car, or get where we want to go, by looking in our rear view mirror. That is absurd.

But it is important that we take time to glance back; to observe what is happening and change course if need be.

Our past can be a gift to us. It can tell us many things:

- about ourselves,

- about our decisions that continue to influence our future,

- about our behaviors and thoughts that keep us from going where we really want to go.

Philosopher Soren Kierkegaard said, *"Life can only be understood backwards; but it must be lived forwards."* [4]
So...keep the rear view mirror in perspective. It's small for a reason. But it's also there for a reason.

What is the gift you see today in your rear view mirror? Don't neglect the gift!

5 It Happened On A Sunday!

Leisha's version:

Daddy was the children's pastor (actually singles and worship Pastor--but sometimes they seemed like big kids!) at Calvary at the time. It was a dedication Sunday. If you don't know what a dedication Sunday is, it is a Sunday that parents dedicate their babies to the church and to God. Dad was the one in charge of it. Except he was with his wife at the hospital having one of their own! ME!

My version:

I remember this day like I do the births of my other two girls. My telling of the story usually begins when the first labor pains began. Cait and Brie will humor me by saying, "Ok Mom, what time was it when...?" as if they know my need to remember it all. But Leisha would settle in next to me and ask, "and then what did I do?"

She was born on a Sunday! It just happened to be THE Sunday that our church was dedicating a brand new sanctuary. Rennie was overseeing all the music and helping with the child dedication at the end of the service. But 45 minutes before the service began, I had to call him to tell him it was time. I couldn't wait at home anymore. And just as the church family witnessed the final moment of dedication, when parents dedicated their child to the Lord, Leisha made her way into our family.

It was 12:16pm! April 28, 1991.

Yep! This is one of those stories. It is the birth story I replay every year on the birthday of each of my girls. It's the story that comes up every time I am with a soon to be mother and we get to talking about 'the birth'.

No, I don't have to include this for all to read, but with Leisha's death comes a very deep desire to remember the day she was born. She lived here with me. I carried her in my womb, I gave her birth. I longed to love her as she could feel love.

But it is more than that. There is something important about recalling the day you were born, or remembering the events of your child's birth and reconnecting to the dreams you had for them.

I know not everyone has a birth experience that is full of love. Some babies have been put up for adoption without ever feeling their birth mothers' arms around them. Some children were born into a home that treated them as trophies, or worse yet, obligations, not to mention the abuse that happens to so many children. You have heard the battle I had with God before Leisha was born. I get it. It's not always pretty.

But when Leisha finally came, I was very much in love with this little being making her way into our world.

The labor pains started around 1:00am. This was my third baby, I was determined I would not go to the hospital too soon. So I got up around 1:30am to walk through the contractions. I paced the distance of the family room over and over--sometimes able to sit and read. I don't remember being tired. There was an excitement knowing this baby was coming...and soon.

I kept whispering to the top of my belly, "You can't come right away. Your daddy has to be at church this morning. They are dedicating the new auditorium at church and your daddy is in charge of it all." I kept saying we needed to wait until this afternoon, but my body continued to indicate she was not listening.

About 3:30am Rennie noticed I hadn't come back to bed so he came to investigate. He talked me through a few contractions, which began to gain strength so that I couldn't do anything but 'lean' into them and breathe it out.

As he saw the intensity grow, Ren, too, was concerned about his commitments. He dressed and took off for church about 6:30am and my mom took over the labor watch.

By 9:30, I called the doctor and filled him in on the timing of the contractions. I hadn't wanted to go too early, but...I didn't want to wait too long either. Doc agreed.

I called Ren.

In just a few minutes, a service that involved months of planning and hundreds of people was supposed to begin. Here I am calling him to say his baby was coming! I wondered if he would be able to get here in time. Our dear friends, Cindy and Gary, heard the news and coached him out the door. We were at the hospital by 10:15am. Someone else would have to lead the service he had spent weeks planning.

"You've got a long way to go yet!" the doctor said at the first check. "Get settled in!" But this was not my first baby and I sensed things were happening faster than he thought. Sure enough! A half hour later, at my request he checked again. "Whoa! She's on her way! Let's do this!"

At 12:16pm, April 28th, 1991, she was born.

Fifteen minutes after the Dedication Service at church was over, we were together celebrating a new life in our own family--our third daughter.

****

Each person's life is a story with a beginning, a middle, and an end. The value of connecting with our beginning is part of understanding the *tale we fell into*, the heritage we were born into, and the legacy of those who came before. These are all signals of some of the themes that will play out in our life. They are part of the journey we each take to find the answer to the question, *Who Am I?*

But it is more than that! We are not just finding ourselves, but God!

I appreciate these thoughts from Dan Allender, in his book *To Be Told*,

Most people don't know how to read their life in a way that reveals their story. They miss the deeper meaning in their life, and they have little sense of how God has written their story to reveal himself and his own story.[1] (pg 1)

Think about that! Not only is God our Creator as he formed us in the womb and knew every day of our life before a single day had passed. (Psalm 139:13-16) He is also the Author of our life. He is using every person's unique story to tell his Divine story.

When we recognize, as Leisha did, that our story is not just a random series of happenings, and that each event or person in it is part of a much bigger plot, we begin to understand that we are much more than just a character in the story. We have the potential to be *a writer of our future,* as Allender puts it. We have the privilege of taking all that God has given us: our design, our dreams, our experiences, and turning them into a story that reflects him to others in our world.

We are not *just surviving*, or getting through our days. We are aware that in each day our stories:
- point us to God.
- invite us to notice him.
- allow us to reflect him.

I chose to tell Leisha about Baby Eric and the battle I had with God before she was born. It was part of her heritage that I felt was important for her to know. While it hurt me to read her words in chapter 1, I was thrilled that she caught the outcome of that wrestling match. Leisha wrote,

Mom knew that God was going to use this baby (me) and even as hard as it was for her to accept it, she did. And I was born.

Yes! Why God let Leisha live and Baby Eric die that year, I don't know. But there was no doubt in my mind that God was going to use this little girl. I often saw signs of how he was using her; in my life, with her Dad and her sisters, with her friends.

At Leisha's birth, we announced her to the world by calling her our MAJOR 3rd. I loved the musical metaphor because I had pursued a major in church music in college, and worked with choirs and music groups most of my life. I was the oldest of five kids of a very musical family. We all sang, played piano and another instrument, and joined our parents in family presentations all over our local community.

When I knew Rennie and I were having our third girl, I couldn't resist advertising a little trio of our own.

Even as young girls, I taught them one of the songs I had used with my first children's choir. As I sang through it again recently, I was grateful that it spoke so clearly of God's presence in their life, *even before they were born. (Even Before I Was Born* by Tina English)[2]

Even Before I was Born, God knew my name.
Even before I was born, he had a plan.
Even before I met mom and dad,
there was something special 'bout me!
Even before I could cry, "I'm here!"
He knew that I was meant to be.

Even before I was born, I had a place,
Even though I didn't know, he picked my race.
Even before I began to grow he had held me in his hand.
Somehow he knew where I'd be today,
And that's my part of God's plan.

Even before I was born, God knew my name,
The number of hairs on my head,
the fact that none of them are the same
Even before the day of my birth
there was something special 'bout me!
The color of my eyes and the way that I smiled
He knew that I was meant to be.

6 What Shall We Name Her

Leisha's version:
So April 28th, 1991, on a Sunday afternoon in Honeybrook, Pennsylvania at Brandywine Hospital, they had a little baby girl named Leisha Danae Burrus.

My version:
Choosing a name for a third daughter was a bigger challenge than I thought it would be. Everything in me would have loved to wait to name my children until I had a chance to get to know them a little--maybe even as long as 2 or 3 years. I wanted to be sure we had the right name for the person they were--not one we snatched out of a book somewhere.

Dan Allender, in *To Be Told (pg. 29)* speaks to that mindset.

> *"In the ancient Near East a name conferred meaning and a future to be lived up to or lived down. A **name marked a person** with a set of expectations that determined that person's place in the family and in the world. Today it is rare that parents first study a child in order to give the child a name that fits. Far more often, we choose a name that sounds good and has meaning that we like. The Hebrew process of naming was exactly opposite. A name was chosen that **reflected the unique calling and character of the child.** It is for this reason that many Bible characters were renamed later in life."* [1]

But we needed to name our baby before we left the hospital, so we chose a name that sounded good to us and had meaning for us.

Our first born daughter got the 'privilege', or probably better said, burden of being named after her parents. Caitlin was for Kathlyn (meaning *Pure One)* and Renee for Rennie (which meant *Reborn).* At the time, we thought Caitlin was a rather unique name, but it turned out there were 6 other Caitlin's in the hospital nursery at the same time--all spelled a little different; some were first names, some middle names. Sorry honey!

Cait was born in Plano, Texas, while Rennie was finishing his Master of Theology degree from Dallas Seminary. I had been teaching elementary music at the time and she was known to dance to the music while still in the womb. It was indeed a special trip back to the elementary school after she was born. All the kids were so excited to see her.

The name of our second child was picked out when we still lived in Texas before I even had thoughts of my own kids. On a trip to visit my sister in Pennsylvania, I had fallen in love with a beautiful babe named Brielle. I had never heard the name before, and had promised that one day I would name a blond haired, blue eyed daughter Brielle. Brielle is a form of the name Gabrielle which means *God is my Strength.* Her middle name is RaeAnn using the middle names of Ren's parents. Ray means counsel or protection. Ann is gracious and merciful. We called her Breezy for short!

As it turned out, Ren and I had moved to the same area of Pennsylvania between Caitlin and Brielle's birth. Our Brielle was born in the same hospital as her namesake. The nurse caring for us after our daughter's birth said, "I have a niece with that name. How did you decide on that?" I told her when and where I met the precious babe years earlier. Her eyes got bigger and bigger! "That's my Brielle you are describing! The baby you named your Brielle after is my niece." Who would have ever imagined! We got special treatment from that nurse the rest of our stay!

But for the third child, all the names we had left were boy's names that we hadn't used with the other two. Early in the pregnancy we found out this baby would be a girl.

One thought was to use the name Lee. A special aunt and uncle that had mentored both Ren and I through college were named **Le**land and Rosa**lie**. So we thought we could use the spelling LEI--so that it would be a bit different. And No! We didn't know about the clothing line then called L.E.I. (stands for Life, Energy and Intelligence.) I dug out all the baby name books I could find (we didn't have internet then) to see what names we could use that had LEI in them. Many were nice--none were quite right.

One morning a couple of weeks before our baby was born, I woke up with a vivid memory. I had spent much of my life working with kids and youth music, especially just before Caitlin was born. This particular morning I recalled a musical written by Michael W. Smith and Andy Stanley called *The Big Picture: A Youth Musical about God's Providence.*[2] It is the story of a group of young people who are dealing with two of their group being in a tragic car accident. The boy was in the hospital. The girl had been killed. Her name was Leesha.

In the musical, while the kids in the youth group are asking questions, the boy lying in a hospital bed is also grappling with why Leesha died and he lived. Counter to that are scenes of Leesha in heaven asking some of the same questions.

- Why do bad things happen to good people?
- Why was Leesha taken when she was so sold out to the Lord?

- She was making such a difference. Why would God allow this to happen?

They asked age old questions and learned big lessons about Providence and the Big Picture that God sees and we don't.

I was challenged by this musical from the very first time I heard it. Leesha had made the kind of difference I wanted to make myself as a teenager. If I died, I hoped people would speak of me as one who knew God and pointed others to him. I wanted then, as I do even now, to make a difference with my life. There needed to be more Leeshas in the world.

But this Leesha had made much of her influence after she died. One of the songs in the musical is called *I Hear Leesha*. The kids in youth group are pondering her death. The words go like this:

I HEAR LEESHA.

Seems like it was only yesterday
She was living here
Yeah, she was living here

Lord knows why He's taken her away
It isn't very clear
No, it isn't very clear

Into every life a little rain must fall
And losing one you love is like a storm
But storms are passing

I hear Leesha singing in Heaven tonight
And in between the sadness
Oh, I hear Leesha telling me that she's alright

Life goes on even after life
And that's what I believe
Yea, that's what I believe

Woh, Leesha's gone but she will still survive
In a memory that I'm keeping
Here with me

Silencing the voice of mortal tragedy
Listening to whispers of the soul
All is peaceful

I hear Leesha singing in Heaven tonight
And in between the sadness
Oh, I hear Leesha telling me that she's alright

Into every life a little rain must fall
And losing one you love is like a storm
But storms are passing

I hear Leesha singing in Heaven tonight
In between the sadness
Oh, I hear Leesha telling me that she's alright
I hear Leesha singing in Heaven tonight
In between the sadness
Oh, I hear Leesha telling me that she's alright

By Michael W Smith and Wayne Kirkpatrick

Used with permission. 3

Something inside me knew someone needed to take that Leesha's place.

But I specifically begged God, *"Please never let me be sorry I did this! I never want to use that song at my daughter's funeral."*

****

A name is a precious gift. In my years of working with people, I have watched what happens when I use someone's name to greet them. I'm one of those personalities that might greet a friend with, "Hey Beautiful!" or "Hi sweet lady!" They almost always smile and interact with me.

But when I call someone by their name, they love it! Often they take a second look at me, eyes looking directly into my eyes, as if to return the favor. I see them, I call them by name. They make new effort to see me back.

I remember a conversation with my friend Barbara as she confided in me that she loved her name. When I, or other people, greeted her with a generic term, such as *sweet lady,* she felt as generic as the term. For instance, many ladies are sweet, at least to someone like me that uses the phrase often.

But when I called her Barbara, I saw her! Sure there are other Barbara's, like my dear mother-in-law. But my saying her name affirmed that I knew who I was talking to. And I cared enough to use her name and made the effort to do so.

Years ago Rennie took the Dale Carnegie class called *How to Win Friends and Influence People.* One of the primary things they were taught was how to remember a person's name. I remember thinking with pride at the time that I already did that pretty well. I loved people, I loved learning their names.

But as the class was finishing, Ren invited me to a social function event with the group. One by one the class members came to me and said, "Kathy, it is so great to meet you!" We had never met! But they had gone the extra mile and learned the names of each class member's spouses too!

I felt noticed.
I felt known.
I felt like I belonged.
I felt like I needed to work harder to know their names.

Our name is our identity. It is another part of reminding us who we are.

But knowing our name, and how we came by that name, and the meaning of the given name, doesn't mean it is the name we live by.

Over the course of our life, we come up with all kinds of names besides the one on our birth certificate. Some are good and cause us to live up to our name; others only speak into the negative talks we have with ourselves.

- You're not good enough.
- Why would anyone want to work with you?
- What do you have to offer anyway?

If we aren't careful, we can be so good at telling ourselves who we aren't that we lose all courage to be who we are.

Instead we compare ourselves to the names of others: beautiful wife, perfect mom, owner of her own business, and excellent housekeeper to boot! So we think we must be like *so and so* and we work *oh so* hard to become all the things that are true about someone else.

The problem comes when we begin to compare our insides with their outsides. We know all the stuff going on in our world. We are aware of every fault and weakness that we live out. But all we see from others is what is on the outside, which we are all pretty good at masking to look good.

Not to mention that we are nothing like that *other woman*.
She has a gift of administration; you have the gift of helps.
She has an ability to speak publicly, you love behind the scenes.
She has just lost her job and had to create a business to live.
You don't need to do that--wouldn't want to do that and if you are honest, are grateful every day that you can do what you already do.

Why do we get caught up comparing our name and our lives to someone else's, and insisting what they offer is better than what we offer the world? We spend much of our life discontented and dissatisfied with our contribution.

What if we discovered who we are and lived out our own design? What if we celebrated *other women* to be exactly who they are too?

Truth be owned, you being ordinary you is extraordinary to *the other women* in your world.

Having all girls, we read and watched a lot of the Anne of Green Gables series. One of my favorite scenes in Anne of Avonlea was a conversation between Anne and her kindred spirit friend Diana. Anne's response was priceless,

> *"That's a lovely idea, Diana," said Anne enthusiastically. "Living so that you beautify your name, even if it wasn't beautiful to begin with...making it stand in people's thoughts for something so lovely and pleasant that they never think of it by itself."*
> – L.M. Montgomery, *Anne of Avonlea* [4]

What if we lived so that we beautified our name? How would life be different if we embraced all the richness of who we are? What if we lived it so completely that when others heard our name they immediately knew our loveliness?

Leisha used a lot of ink and paper writing her name over and over again. Even to this day, I'll thumb through a leftover tablet or notebook and find her name written a dozen different ways. One of her favorite things to do was to create an acrostic for her name like this one.

> L is for life, which is short so live well.
> E is for enjoy, your life can be fun!
> I is for influence, your purpose for living.
> S is for special, you are and so is your friend
> H is for hand, that you always give.
> A is for attractive, inside and out!

I have had people tell me that these exercises of playing with your name and identifying characteristics that you want to be true of you are "pie in the sky" futility. One woman said, "We end up saying things that aren't true to try and convince ourselves we are better than we are."

Another woman told me, "God just wants us to be quiet and faithful at the things he puts in our path". That works for her. It is exactly who she seems to be. Everything about her has a stillness to it. It was when she inserted a "that's how I do it, you should too!" that I challenged her.

When we expect others to be like we are or demand that we behave like others, we are discrediting the unique design God gave us.

Romans 12: *³For by the grace given me I say to every one of you: Do not think of yourself more highly than you ought, but rather think of yourself with sober judgment, in* *accordance with the faith God has distributed to each of you. ⁴ For just as each of us has one body with many members, and these members do not all have the same function, ⁵ so in Christ we, though many, form one body, and each member belongs to all the others. ⁶ We have different gifts, according to the grace given to each of us.⁵*

So on the one hand we *shouldn't think more highly* of ourselves than we ought. On the other hand, we *should think as highly* of ourselves as we ought. Recognizing our appropriate name, as well as the names of others allows us all to be part of 'belonging' with one another. And when we know who we are, we are much more clear and effective at being who we were made to be in each other's lives.

We often had nicknames for the girls: Cait Babe, Breezy Boop, or Leisha Girl. But in Leisha's journal she had written in big bold letters: B.A.B.E.

B- Beautiful
A- Accepted
B- Blessed
E- Eternally significant

This was not original to Leisha, since I discovered these same terms used by a ministry that conducts events around the country for young women called B.A.B.E. The author, Andrea Stephens (www.andreastephens.com) has explained B.A.B.E. in her book called, *Girlfriend, You are a B.A.B.E.*⁶ I'm guessing Leisha found it in Focus on the Family's BRIO magazine and just entered it into her journal.

But...if you were living to beautify your name, no matter what age you are, this would be a great way to do it.

Beautiful:
> You have been hand crafted by the Master Creator. In his eyes you are absolutely gorgeous. That's right. No more pressure to look like an airbrushed cover girl. You are already beautiful! But that's not all. You also have the potential to feel beautiful. Feeling breathtaking is determined by your actions. Truly attractive girls are those who serve others. Doing something good for someone else is what God-defined beauty is all about.

Accepted:
> You are accepted. No strings attached. God's approval of you isn't based on performance, grades, I.Q, clothes, popularity, weight or shade of lip gloss. Though you will experience rejection of classmates or teammates, the King of kings is giving you a holy thumbs up! You are accepted just because you are his! So forget trying to please everyone else. Who cares how the other girls and guys score you! As an authentic B.A.B.E you can focus on the Lord and base your value on what the Bible says about you.

Blessed:
> You are the proud owner of countless spiritual blessings that no one can take away from you. And you've been showered with spiritual gifts and special abilities given by God's Spirit. As you intentionally identify and develop your gifts, you will have so much fun seeing how you can be effective for the Lord every day. That brings us to the last letter.

Eternally Significant:
> You are here on Earth at this very time in history for a reason. Your life is not about nothingness. It's about involving yourself in God's eternal plan and purpose. You can even increase your heavenly assignments by purposely preparing to be the kind of B.A.B.E whom God can use by

studying his Word. God has exciting plans for you, girlfriend! Your spiritual gifts, special abilities, personality, and passions will all work together in a role God designed for you and only you. You can make a difference in your generation and glorify God at the same time. You honor God with your life and live his purpose for you.[6]

As I read these words in Leisha's own handwriting, I marveled.

When we named Leisha our criteria was:
1. find a name a little different than current popular names.
2. use our appreciation for the LEE's in our life.
3. raise up a LEESHA to make a difference in her world.

But even at a young age, God was already showing up to teach Leisha that her name, who she was, and what she was made to be, was about so much more.

PERFECT LITTLE LIVES

7 Mom, I'm throwing Up!

Leisha's version:
So there they are, happy little family in a yellow house while the man of the house is off being a great assistant pastor and his perfect pastor's daughters and his perfect pastor's wife are home playing and growing and having a grand old time being perfect (or trying anyway).

My version:
My heart wrenched with the word "perfect". Was she right? Were we trying to live 'perfect little lives' even before she was born? I know we did after. We became keenly aware that our drive to be a 'good little pastor's family' was about to do all of us in. But I was grieved as I read Leisha's description of us 'trying' to be perfect. Even more troubling was the awareness she had that she somehow 'messed up our world' when she was born into it.

I pondered all Ren and I brought to our love story:
Both of us were first- born children.
Both were leaders and comfortable being up-front and on teams.
Both of us had trusted Christ as our Savior and knew God had a plan for our lives.
Both of us were passionate or driven. There was some debate as to which term was the correct description.

I loved people and Ren loved tasks.
We had goals for making a difference and were doing what
we could to reach them.

I had to admit we started this marriage with a desire to do it
right. I never equated that with having 'perfect little lives?' In
fact, I worked really hard to not go there. As a Pastor's kid, I
knew what that could look like and I thought I was working hard
to do it "well", not perfect.

So when did it all get so out of control?

I hesitate to write these next pages. Offering them here is a risk.
What will you think of me if I tell of the places in our lives we
didn't have it all together? What if I take off the mask enough for
you to see me as I really am?

But to not include these pages is to leave out the intense training
we received in the REAL LIFE BOOT CAMP. That was the place
we began to understand in a new way that God was big enough
in the raw, messy, real world we live in.

So it is with trembling hand, and the blessing of my family that I
continue to write these parts of our story.

Leisha was one–year- old when we moved from that yellow
house in Pennsylvania to a little white house at the edge of
Pandora, OH. Rennie had accepted a position as pastor of youth
and families at St. John Mennonite Church.

The emotions had been pretty high the day we moved. It may
have been more so for mom and dad than the girls, but they felt
it. I remember vividly as we drove through the Ohio state line,
the sign over the interstate said, *'Ohio, the heart of it all!"* I had

a strong sense that many aspects of our former life would be converging at this church in the cornfields of northwest Ohio.

Caitlin was just starting kindergarten when we moved. She had loved public school, especially her teachers, but since she was little she had asked if we could homeschool. In Pennsylvania, we had a co-op one day a week with a girlfriend. One week I had her son (which she deemed the same effort as my two oldest girls), and she had a day to run errands. The next week she had my girls, I could get some things done at home. Cait loved it and thrived in that environment. But I was determined she would go to school, or maybe it was more that I would not homeschool.

But a year and a half later we moved to the tall brick house out in the country where I am writing from today and we started homeschooling when Cait was in the 2nd grade. It wasn't because I thought I could do it better than the schools (I struggled with inadequacy all the years we homeschooled), but because I had an opportunity to be with my kids, to teach, encourage, laugh, study, play each day. With a great homeschool support group in the area, I was willing to try.

Growing up as a preacher's kid, I was very aware of the stereotypes that could be put on the children of the pastor. I worked hard to let my kids be kids and tried in every way possible not to even hint they needed to be perfect.

They wore pretty little dresses that often matched, compliments of Grandy Burrus!

The girls learned early our family liked to sing. Occasionally we would be asked to sing for church. I would go to the piano; Rennie would kneel down by the girls with a microphone until they got old enough to hold it themselves.

Then sometimes they would sing trios, or Cait would play her violin while the other two sang. Or one would play for the offering. My favorite times when they got older were when we would do a women's quartet. I loved being able to add my voice to theirs. Their piano teacher, Christy, would often play for us.

Many people worried about their socialization, but they actually had so many opportunities to be social that it was a challenge to keep on track with the school work. They took part in church and community events. Caitlin and Leisha had been part of the Lima youth orchestra, and they all took piano and violin lessons. Brie took trumpet for a while. They played basketball for the Ohio Heat Eagles, the local homeschool team. They were in plays and a few musicals.

Leisha also took debate. That changed all our worlds. Now not only was Leisha bold enough to take us on in our discussions-- especially with her dad, but she could begin to think through both sides of the debate and come up with a winning argument.

In 2003, Rennie became the lead pastor, and though we were still homeschooling, as the girls got older, I got more involved at church helping coordinate the worship services with Christy. (Yes, she was also the piano teacher.) We were in the process of experiencing some pretty phenomenal things at church. At least it felt like it would be significant.

At a point of re-evaluation of the purpose of our church, the leadership had taken inventory of where the church was and felt like we were ready to address some next steps. We had high hopes that it was an extremely forward movement. And the elders and staff seemed united on the direction.

So much great stuff was happening! Then...not so much!

****

It was a beautiful Saturday in July of 2003 when Brielle called me into her room. I was glad for the moment. I had wanted to talk with her about some things I was noticing.

"Mom, I'm throwing up."

I sat on the edge of her bed, trying to allow the words to sink in. I had suspected for a while that she was struggling. I was waiting for the right time to sit her down and talk about it. Having worked with the Minirth-Meier Psychiatric Clinic in Dallas while Rennie was in seminary, specifically in the adolescent unit, I had watched other parents walk with their daughters through some painful places with eating disorders. I also knew my daughter needed to be willing to address the issues with us. But now finally hearing her say it, my heart began to absorb what she was really saying.

We knew Brie's illness was not just hers. Her issue shed light on problems we were all dealing with in one way or another. Her words steered us to a path so different than we thought we were going to be on right then. It was a huge awakening as we were going into something big at the church that was going to address some *un-health* and next steps to wholeness. Now as a family, we were embarking on a journey that would address our own issues.

Each of us felt a chaos we couldn't fully control, so we took control of what we could. For some it was our appearance, our good work, our good attitude, our success at doing our work and reaching our goals. During this time, we immersed ourselves in our work, our studies, good books, music and activity.

Each one of us screamed to be noticed for who we really were; not what role we played or whose daughter we were. Often it was to escape the 'noise' of a family saying much but mostly clamoring for a space to be heard. Caitlin so poignantly captured the struggle in her poem called *WORDS* [1] (Poem is included at the end of this chapter.) as she so aptly described the noise that our family made--everyone talking, no one listening.

Even as I write, I feel the ache. I was trying desperately to DO the right thing; to take the next right step with the right intention and attitude at home, with school work, and at church. I thought I was doing that.

After all I was consumed with 'the Lord's work'.

Even before our first date, Rennie felt a desire to be involved in the pastorate. I totally got that and empowered him as best I could to do what was needed at church. I felt called to ministry too. At the age of 13, I committed my life to serve the Lord full time in some way. Rennie understood and supported me as he could.

We both believed our girls were our first and most important relationship and responsibility. And we thought we were doing that too.

Somewhere along the line, we taught the girls we were about *"God's business"*, and God came first, right? They had been at church every time we needed to be there when they were younger. As they got older, they wanted the freedom to choose if they would be at church or not. Sometimes we were able to let them make that choice. Other times we insisted they join us for whatever was going on.

Slowly church became "not safe". It was robbing them of the parents they so desperately longed for. God's voice is the voice to heed, right? But we failed to recognize that God uses the voices of those who love us to speak into our lives too.

It was imperative that we listen.

Our perfect little lives began to unravel.

****

We knew that ED, as we came to call the eating disorder, was not just the issue of one family member. Our girls were struggling to keep up with us, each one in a hard place, partly trying to protect us, partly hiding their own emotions. This was an issue that affected all of us, so we began family counseling.

Rennie and I met with Dr. Barnes. The girls met with Jane, a true answer to prayer. Jane was a young counselor completing an internship, counseling under the supervision of a clinical psychologist on staff. The girls loved her, and she really invested in them, probably more than a counselor should have. But we needed that right then.

As I think about it now after having completed my own training as a coach, I have had many discussions about how important it is to keep a distance from the emotions of my client. To carry them all would make me useless for anyone. But at that moment we needed Jane to carry the burden with us. Her involvement was so significant. I am just so grateful she was there, at that point in her journey and ours. She and Dr. B both had wrestled with pain in their own story that would now help us understand the pain we were experiencing.

For our first session we all met together downstairs in the community room. Our counselors instructed us that we were going to be making family sculptures. Each of us would arrange the other family members in a way that best depicted what our family currently looked like.

The girls went first. The sad thing is I don't remember how the girls positioned us. It was the beginning of our awareness how much we weren't listening to them.

When it was my turn, I positioned Ren down like he was a football player at the line with the ball while I stood behind him. I thought I was positioning him so he could make the play. But as I look at it now, perhaps I wanted to call the play.

I placed the girls behind us: Cait standing tall in the middle, Brie and Leisha on each side leaning out slightly. All of them had arms stretched out creating a fan. They were the cheerleaders to back us up and cheer us on.

Even as I was placing each one and finally taking my place, I sensed this wasn't what I wanted it to be, but it spoke what was. So unhealthy! I wasn't looking at the girls at all, and I'm looking over Rennie. We ended up looking like an over-performing turkey.

When it was Rennie's turn, he positioned all of us doing our favorite things. He SAW us where we loved to be. I was amazed. I was at the piano with a pencil behind my ear arranging a new song. Brie was lying on the floor with her sketch-pad. Cait had her nose in a book reading. Leisha was perched at the computer, exploring.

He had us all in our favorite places. It meant so much to me. He sees who we are!

And then the counselors asked him where he was. "I'm in the kitchen by myself, doing the dishes because THEY aren't doing their jobs."

I felt the slap across the face. I watched as all three of the girls sank in their places.

86

He saw us! But he didn't like who we were. He didn't think we were doing the right thing.

His love language was acts of service. None of us were doing that for him. He saw us doing what we loved, but he wasn't able to be where he loved to be, because he felt like he had to cover for us-- for me! He was doing what needed to be done because it needed to be done. It was the right thing to do.

Wow! That one counseling session seemed to open up huge awareness.
- We're not listening to the girls
- None of us were doing well, and it started with Ren and me.

Getting to healthy was going to take a lot of hard work: emotionally, mentally, physically and even spiritually. Am I willing to do what it takes? What does healthy look like anyway?

Words, by Caitlin Renee Burrus, December 2003[1]

Words

Always words.

Painful words,

Pointless words,

Endless words,

People crying,

Voices begging,

Humans shouting,

Angry, hurtful, selfish, desperate,

Always wanting to be heard

Above the rest.

And so the noise rises.

Quiet, my soul longs for quiet,

My heart for rest,

My mind for peace,

Yet, I am shouting just as loud,

I am a part of the noise,

When will we learn to listen,

To love,

To slow down and see,

To taste,

To smell,

To hear.

When will we learn that less is more.

When will we stop wanting all

And be content

With what we have,

Who we are.

When will we learn that Christ is all

And we are not.

How long must voices cry

In pain and despair

Before we see the light.

Why must it take so long?

We are deaf,

And so the noise rises.

Hope, there is always hope,

Only look to the light.

The Son came to earth,

The light to the dark,

But we put it out.

We cried for light

But when it came it hurt our eyes,

So we killed it.

But the light came back

With love,

With hope,

We were scared

And ran away.

We were angry

And blocked it out,

We were selfish

And did not want to give up

what we had

For the light, the hope,

And so the noise rises.

But there is always hope,

Always light,

Always love,

Always arms waiting,

All we have to do is ask

And the dark flees,

Hope returns,

And though the noise may not end,

We will stop joining in,

We can show others our hope

and then, one day,

all may be silent in awe of the light.

The dark will flee.

Hope returns.

And the loving arms of our Savior

Welcome us home.

There is always hope

In the Son of God,

Jesus Christ.

He is our light.

> *"Sooner or later, all people suffer loss, in little doses or big ones, suddenly or over time, privately or in public settings. Loss is as much a part of normal life as birth, for as surely as we are born into this world, we suffer loss before we leave it."[1]*

No, these are not Leisha's words. They were written by a man named Jerry Sittser in his book called *A Grace Disguised*. Years ago, at the third anniversary of a tragic accident that took the lives of his wife, his mother and his 4 year old daughter, he penned these words. I knew if this man could speak truth, WITH HOPE, just 3 years after that depth of brokenness, I wanted to hear what he had to say!

> *It is not, therefore, the experience of loss that becomes the defining moment of our lives, for that is as inevitable as death.... It is HOW WE RESPOND to loss that matters. That response will largely determine the quality, the direction, and the impact of our lives... it is possible to live in and be enlarged by loss, even as we continue to experience it."[2]*

How should we respond? Could it be that simple and yet that hard all at the same time? It's not the losses we were experiencing, but the way we responded to those losses. My broken road had much to teach me about what Jerry meant when he said, *"it is how we respond that matters."* I had plenty of opportunities to respond!

If I pulled out my Life Map of this time in our lives, you would see it was a season of ups and downs--very intense, dramatic ups and downs.

For one thing, we were with our daughters in family counseling in the fight of our lives.

For another, ministry at church had become so intense. Two key staff members left. We were now in the process of rebuilding the leadership team which involved a great deal of re-evaluation and re-structuring. It was good for the church, but it was difficult to work through.

All during this time, I had been significantly struggling with my health. In March 2003, I noticed for the first time that I was getting a great 'tan', but I wasn't tanning. I also noticed my clothes were fitting better, but I wasn't dieting. We all know trying to lose weight is never that easy!

Over the next year, I got darker, and lost more weight. I looked good! But my fatigue increased. I was exhausted all the time and found it very difficult to climb the two flights of stairs to our attic bedroom.

Yet I felt like I had to keep going. These were some of the most trying days of ministry we've ever experienced. With everything going on at church and with our family, I couldn't stop! Or at least I didn't know where to say no.

But late February 2004, right after the Sunday morning worship services, I did stop! More accurately, I collapsed. The girls found me in Rennie's office. Ren carried me to the car, drove me home and put me to bed. For the next month, I slept.

Finally in late March, through a series of visits with doctors, I was pointed to an endocrinologist. Within minutes at our first meeting I was diagnosed with Addison's disease. My adrenal glands had quit functioning. They handle our 'fight or flight' ability to deal with stresses--good or bad. I had plenty of both at the time.

The doctor gave me a shot of cortisol and said, "Girl, in a few hours you'll be feeling much better." I doubted it would be that soon, but it was! Within 12 hours, I felt like I had been resurrected, death now coming to life. I went from feeling gingerbread flat to becoming 3-dimensional again as I felt the blood begin to course through my veins, and the strength return to my body. I was resurrected; my whole being was coming to life!

It was that very evening some girlfriends from church came to visit. We had all been part of a team that traveled to Ukraine the year prior to lead worship at a women's conference. They were surprised to find me sitting up. They saw pink in my face again and a bit of a sparkle in my eye. Another friend prepared a thanksgiving feast for us that evening. She didn't know what had happened, but I knew God had arranged this moment for us to celebrate. I was full of thanks. It was the first time I had eaten a meal in months.

How could it be after months of struggling to live, I could suddenly feel LIFE? I was far from healthy, but this felt really good.

My response: gratitude and thanksgiving!

****

REMUDA:

In August, we realized Brielle was struggling more again with ED, her eating disorder. Brie and Counselor Jane began to talk with us about an eating disorder treatment center in Arizona called Remuda Ranch. We were familiar with it having referred several other families there in the past.

"Mom," Brie pleaded, "I need to go away! I can't do what I need to do at home." We agreed.

So Ren and I flew with our 15-year-old daughter to a place we knew, from the experience of others, could be a healing place. We were picked up at the airport. They gave us the 50 cent tour of the facilities, had us sign her paperwork and then said, "Time to say goodbye!" Within an hour, we were returned to the hotel, our emotions raw and fragile with pain. She would be gone for 2 months. From now on, Brie had to earn the right to even talk with us.

During the time Brie was at Remuda, we had one call a week with her and her Remuda counselor. We would turn on the speaker-phone on the kitchen counter, and lean over it to talk to Brie. Now, in the pain of this moment, we were turned toward each other, huddled around a phone that connected us to the one family member not in our circle.

It was the kitchen counter, especially after Brie came back, where we gathered around to eat a meal or share a story. Sometimes it happened at the table. But most often when the girls would come home from basketball, or Ren would come home from work, we would gather around the counter with a snack and share the goings-on of the day. I loved seeing the transformation taking place in how we did family times.

As we became healthier and more vulnerable, sharing what was really going on inside and what we thought or felt, our family sculpture was changing for all of us. We were turning inward, facing each other, seeing each other. At important moments of our lives after that, we would huddle up as a family in a small circle, arms wrapped around, fingers touching, heads bowed in as we would pray for the child leaving or the next big step we were making. Precious times! Healing moments!

My response: I tried to keep the counter clear and healthy snacks available. This was a sacred place for family.

****

In October, our whole family was invited to Remuda to spend some time in training to help Brie and the family prepare for her re-entry into our home. By then she had been there 5 weeks. It was a sweet reunion.

We were partnered with 2 other families and much of any given day was filled with counseling and training to help us all live and love honestly through this.

We were led to the horse barn for a rodeo presented by the girls. Each girl was assigned a horse to care for and work with during her stay at the Ranch. Brie's horse was blind in one eye and Brie learned to work with her in a special way to create trust. It was great fun to see Brie ride in the arena with confidence. Her only other exposure to horses was in Texas when Ren and the girls got a chance to ride when we went to see his folks.

On Wednesday we were all invited to the art building. That turned out to be a turning point for our family.

The art therapist gave a quick tour of all the art supplies. The outlet of art had often been an inspiration for Brie, but while at Remuda, Brielle had shared many insights she had gleaned while exploring her creative side. This was where Brie felt most at home, and she was so excited for us to share this specific opportunity with her.

Rennie on the other hand was not! This was like a trip to the dentist for him, and he seldom missed a chance to voice his discomfort about it, desperately hoping to get out of it somehow. Yet knowing his involvement was important, for Brie's sake if nothing else, compelled him to participate.

Our instructions were simple: use any supplies available and create something that shows how the eating disorder has affected you.

Hmmm?

Brie and the other resident girls jumped to their feet and headed toward one cubicle or another gathering supplies. Leisha soon followed Brie's lead and Cait was not far behind. Slowly other family members went exploring and soon returned to the tables to work.

It took a little while for me to land on a thought. I looked at some cubicles with beads, or paint, or glue and suddenly felt overwhelmed by the fatigue that threatened at any moment to overtake me. Whatever I did had to be simple! I'll start with paper. I headed for the wall of paper and chose a deep yellow piece of construction paper though I couldn't tell you why at the time. On my way back to the table I grabbed a pencil and scissors, still unsure what I would do with them.

I noticed Rennie, looking so very uncomfortable, still had not moved from his chair.

I pondered! How has this eating disorder affected me? What could I possibly do with this paper, pencil and scissors that could show how conflicted I was inside, how hurt, how guilty, how vulnerable I felt. I opened my scissors and used one blade to make a jagged tear on my yellow page. Yes, that's how it feels; jagged, rough, tearing at the core of my being.

I glanced up to find Rennie now exploring the room. The girls seemed busy on their projects working with purpose. I sketched out the shape of a heart, then more shapes, wondering how each one was answering the charge we had been given. I began to cut out the shapes, but not completely. I left some of them attached a little as if they were dangling. Ah, my heart--trying to be open but feeling more like I'm just out there blown by every strong wind that threatens me. Yep! That's how it feels right now. So detached yet clinging to life as I knew it--or perhaps wanted it to be.

Rennie has returned to his chair; a blank white page lies before him on the table. He is staring at it blankly as well.

I looked back at my yellow page now ripped and cut, images dangling all over. I was struck by the empty holes I now saw. It wasn't right! They shouldn't be empty; they are just different now. I set out for the wall of paper and found a drawer of little scrap pieces in all different colors. I grabbed some pink, blue, orange and red scraps and even a shade of brown. As I walked back to my chair, I looked at the brown, wishing I could put it back. It didn't seem like a good color for my project, and yet, I also marveled I felt that way. With all the hard things that had been going on in our life, you would think I would have started with brown. When life is hard, it feels like it is brown or even black sometimes. But I was only using a little sliver of brown. What was I telling myself about how ED had affected me?

I took a look around the room before I sat down. Every person was showing some degree of creativity; some with big projects made out of Styrofoam and poster board, colored tissue and glue, others working with clay and designing small images to display their emotions. The art therapist was surveying the work and answering questions as needed.

My girls were each focused. Cait looked very intent at her project which included a variety of mediums. Brie was surrounded by paint with paint brush in hand, swirling dark red, orange and yellow across the canvas. Leisha seemed to be in her own world as she worked with clay.

I noticed Rennie now had a ruler and blue pen. He was drawing one long line after another on his white paper. A red pen lay next to him as well. It looked like a piece of notebook paper. Why didn't he just get some notebook paper? Didn't he know there were some lined pages at the paper wall? I was tempted to tell him about it, but knew this was one time I needed to let him be.

I sat down by my yellow page with my scraps and some scotch tape. Hmm? Which side is the front and which is the back? I chuckled under my breath. That is also how the eating disorder feels. You don't know if you are coming or going.

I flipped the paper over and began layering my different colored scraps so that they would show through a shape on the other side. Of course, red was behind the heart, and blue by the rectangle with a star taped to it. It looked like a blue sky with a gold star peering through the window. I taped one scrap down, then another until all the shapes were covered. I observed how messy the back of my page looked now with misshapen pieces of paper taped in all sorts of angles. There was very little of my original yellow sheet still showing.

I turned it over to observe the final outcome. I smiled. My yellow page appeared to be a stained glass window now. Color showed through even behind the jagged lines I had sliced into my page. Each shape now was an opening to SEE more; more of me, more of reality, more of God in that reality, more of my heart.

That had to be part of my answer. My pretty yellow page,

untouched, was my version of my 'perfect little me." I wanted so to portray light and joy, sunshine and all that is good. But life happens and with it comes the jagged edges and the holes that leave openings for ...life! Even the brown piece had its place in my page. All of it part of the bigger work God was doing in my heart.

Ok! I do have something to share! I can SEE how ED has made me ... more!

Our time was up! Now we would share our creations with the other members of our family group. One by one, each person's art-work was set out for others to see. With guidance from our therapist, each individual shared the insights gained as we processed our response to the assignment.

Soon it was our family's turn. One by one we took the hot seat to explain our art.

Leisha was first to present her art. She had made a figurine of a girl out of white clay. The figure was seated with her arms wrapped around bent knees. There were red stripes on the arms, legs and back indicating wounds and on her face were two blue tears. I could see the pain she was describing that was caused by ED, not only Brielle's but hers also. I knew Leisha had been fighting disordered thinking for a long time. She had never gone as far as Brielle had, but it was possible Brie's decision to speak up had saved Leisha from going there.

Then it was my turn to reveal my yellow stain glassed window of sorts, along with all I had already learned. I had to let go of my 'yellow vision for life' and embrace all that was reality. It was only there I would be able to see the beauty that was possible. The therapist indicated she saw what I was feeling.

As I finished and turned to see Brie's presentation, I had full view of Rennie as he sat stoically at the end of the table. I wondered what was going through his mind about now.

Brie had used her talent for art to make many things since she had come to Remuda. She had given some of them to us as gifts when we arrived for Family Week. My favorite was a clay figure of a girl, perhaps an angel in gold standing tall with face lifted and arms stretched down and back. The image spoke of openness and freedom. I knew that was what I was seeing in my daughter's face ever since we first saw her after five weeks. She was beginning to throw her herself open; to take what was and live in each moment with freedom. I rejoiced.

But today her work was a painting of a rose. Brie identified the layers upon layers she had pulled up around herself. Some layers were there to protect herself, others were to hide behind, and still others were trying to create a world she could control. I got her message clearly. I had seen many of those layers come up. I felt responsible for some, helpless with others. But now the rose was beginning to open! It was lovely.

Cait had gone to the paper wall like me, but she had been much more creative. To her big white sheet she had glued a feather and seashells and with it, a picture of a wall. Yes, ED had created a wall, but around it were other things that had been pleasant too. She had been reminded of good that had come through it.

Now it was Rennie's turn. He took a deep breath, pushed his paper out on the table and said, "I've got nothing. My page is blank. I don't have any answers, and I can't fix this thing that is hurting my girl and my family. I don't know what to do! It just makes me feel stupid."

I felt the tears gush from my own eyes and saw Cait and Brie were crying too. Just as I turned to check on Leisha on the other side of me, our artist guide said, "Do you see the response of all the girls in your life?" Ren looked down the row at us. Tears came to his eyes and emotion rose in his voice as he lifted his hands in frustration, "I'm sorry! I don't know what to do!"

The girls surrounded him! 'We know Daddy! You can't fix it! We love you for trying! But now we can do this together. "

Our art class had broken through for all of us in a way we could not have imagined.

Our response was to SEE: Differently than we had seen before, because we allowed ourselves to be in a place we had never been, a place that was not comfortable.

My response: to let go of my 'yellow' life and embrace all the colors and shapes in it--even the brown pieces for the beauty they held. That would become important to remember 2 short years later.

****

The week culminated with what was called our TRUTH IN LOVE session. This was one of the main events during our week at Remuda and the focal point for our counseling since Brie had arrived here. This family therapy session had the goal of *speaking truth in love* for the purpose of understanding, healing, and developing unity as a family.

This was a time we also shared with our family group--two families listened in as the third family sat in a circle in the center of the room. So there we were: Brie facing us, with her counselor by her side. The rest of us were in a semi-circle around her: Cait, Leisha, me, then Rennie.

It started with Brielle making amends for things she felt she had done to hurt us. One by one she faced each of us and repented of something, asking for our forgiveness for each offense. Through her counseling, Brie had prepared a list and was very in tune to things that had caused us pain. I thought I was prepared, but of course the rawness of the moment left me full of emotion with little place to release it except for the tears that managed to escape time and again.

Next we were each given the challenge to address the wounds or offenses we had experienced from the other. Each member of the family was encouraged to use a communication format:

- When you_____.
- I feel _____.
- I need _____.

As we discussed issues we had tiptoed around in our family previously, we were to address the specific, offensive behavior and how it made us feel. But one of the proactive measures was to also identify what it was we needed from the other party. It forced us all to be part of solving the problem, not just complaining about it.

This was followed up with a time of affirmation, each of us celebrating the characteristics we love about one another and the memories we have that we cherish. Much happened in this moment; painful things, sacred things, healing things. As open as I am trying to be in this book, that space was intimately our own. It was precious.

But one thing that did happen during this time was a promise I made to Brielle, Caitlin and Leisha.

"I can't do this right away, but I have listened, and my answer is Yes! It will take until Thanksgiving, but I'll be done with my work at the church by then!"

My response: To open my hands yet again releasing something I thought I wanted. Now I had to go home and make good on my promise.

9 Let It Go!

It was in one of those rare conversations with Brie when we were gathered around the phone on the counter that the topic was first brought up. "Mom, please put 'worship' away. Leave your position at church. It is killing you and us." The words were Brielle's, but I saw in the eyes of the two daughters standing with me that they too longed for me to let go of my part-time job at the church. It took hours longer than it was supposed to, yet was finally paying a few bills.

It was one of those moments when I thought I had it all figured out. I'm doing the right things! I'm 'above and beyond' what I should be doing! I am all right!

And then I saw it--blaring at me in ways that couldn't be more obvious. I fell back on the chair, head in my hands, sometimes tears in my eyes and I realized yet again--I missed it.

TRUTH!

It's the stuff that is really happening in my own heart- and in the behaviors and attitudes of the past few months--and years! It's like I should have known it all along--but I didn't. I didn't want to.

I was angry. In some ways it was because I was beginning to understand my role in all of this. But more than that, I was angry my girls had to ask me to let go and I was hesitating!

They were asking me to walk away from a role I had always dreamed of doing. I had spent my college years training for what I was finally getting to do. It was a position that gave me a platform to both lift the chins of people to see the face of God and empower them to use their gifts and abilities in worship and ministry. I didn't do it perfectly--some would say I didn't do it well. But I knew in my heart I was there because God made me to be there. I was willing to give ALL I had to that end.

Yet, I was giving and giving, and having to fight for every opportunity to do so. Were people influenced by my ministry? Yes! At least some were! But in this moment, I realized I wasn't having the kind of impact at church I longed for. More than that, it was hurting the ones I loved the most in ways I never wanted to hurt them.

When my girls said, "let it go," I knew they were not the only voices I heard asking me to do so. God was speaking too!

"Let it go!"

The counselor asked all of us a single question, "What is the difference between letting go and quitting?"

The girls answered first. I was in awe of their wisdom beyond their years.

Quitting, they said, was giving up. They identified that there was often guilt with quitting. If we start something, we should finish it, especially if a relationship is counting on it.

Hmmm? I knew where they got that! I had heard myself say those very things.

They went on to flesh out what *letting go* was.

Brielle defined it as recognizing you can't do more. It's not about success or failure, being faithful or feeling guilty. It's being committed to the things that are good for you and letting go of the rest.

Leisha created a word picture of putting a boat in a river and 'letting go!' It's a releasing, just as she had to do with her anger toward the eating disorder.

Caitlin agreed with Brie's definition, but she was quick to add that letting go of something that just affects her was easy to do. But when someone else was relying on her to do something, she can't stand to not do it.

Rennie chimed in and summed it up. The difference between letting go and quitting is an attitude of the heart. Both involve relationships, but our attitude toward them is different.

When you quit, you are rejecting something or someone. You say you are done with it, usually with anger and resentment.

When you let go, you say "I've done what I can do. You place it in the Lord's hands, and you walk away from it. "

I pondered that point for a long time. Was I quitting or letting go?

It was one of the most difficult things I had ever done. Not because of what I was walking toward; I knew my family was the more important choice. But it was difficult because it meant letting go of THE *dream* as I knew it to be at that point. It was the best dream I had ever had. Letting go seemed to mean not having a dream--not knowing what to dream next.

But it was very clear. Kathy, let it go!

I was in awe of how hard it was to acknowledge my role at church was contributing to the problem. I felt God had called me to that role, just as he had called me to be their mom.

Now admitting I was part of the problem was so hard. I wasn't present enough. I wasn't paying attention. Is their pain my fault?

There were people at church who told me I was wrong to do what I did. There were others who whispered it to each other in the hallways or parking lots. Still others voiced that I should do it for free as a ministry. If I needed a job, I could go elsewhere, even though the local church had been my passion ever since I could remember.

But still there were many others who sent notes or shared with me that the way I served in my position had given them an opportunity and courage to use their gifts. Others had seen the Lord in their own worship, and that gave life in our Sunday worship settings too. Still others felt a freedom to worship, understanding for the first time that it was not just what we did in a service on Sunday, but how we lived every moment of every day.

In the privacy of my own thoughts one morning, I wrestled. I felt as if I had crawled up on God's lap again and was having it out with him. *Why God?*

- Why did you give me this passion for work in the church, if it was only to be a curse to my precious girls?
- Why make me this way, with these skills and abilities, if using them in the church is wrong?
- Why give me a dream for myself, for my girls and our family, or for this church, only to take it all away?
- Why can't I be both mom and worship leader?

As I voiced the ache in my heart I sensed my hands were fisted, my arms flailing as if I were beating on God's chest as I spoke. I wanted to beat on him. I wanted someone else to blame for what was happening. It can't all be my fault! I was serving you, wasn't I? That can't be all a lie. The last few years of thinking I was hearing your voice can't all be wrong.

I finally grew weary of the battle within me, I fell on to my bed and curled up into a ball with an armful of pillow. When my anger and tears began to subside, a memory flashed into my consciousness.

I was reminded of Ordinary, the main character in Bruce Wilkinson's book, *The Dream Giver*. Our family had read it together on one of our long car trips to Texas.

In the story, Ordinary, a Nobody from the Land of Familiar, left his Usual Job in search of a Big Dream given to him by THE DREAM GIVER.[1] Ordinary faced many obstacles along the way. Discouragement from family and friends, border bullies threatening to scare him back to Familiar and there was even a journey through a Wasteland. Somewhere after that desert place, Ordinary's story was connecting with mine.

I reached for the book that still lay on a bookshelf nearby. I flipped the pages until I found what I was looking for. The page read like this.

> *Ordinary,* said the Dream Giver.
>
> "Yes", said Ordinary.
> *Give me your dream!*
>
> "What do you mean?" Ordinary asked. 'It's my dream. You're the one who gave it to me."

Yes. And now I am asking you to give it back.

Ordinary was shocked, but he didn't have to think. "I can't," he told the Dream Giver. "And I won't!"

...The choice broke his heart![1]

That's where I was--right at that place. My heart was breaking because of this choice. But it hadn't occurred to me God wasn't just asking me to *let it go.* He was asking that I "give it back"!

Yes, he did give me this dream of lifting chins of people to see the face of God.
Yes, he did make me to love music and the making of music to lead others in worship.
Yes, he did use me to help others use their gifts, designs and even their dreams in worship.

But now I heard him ask, "*Give me your dream!*"

Just like Ordinary, I wanted to stomp my foot and scream with everything in me, "It's mine! You gave it to me! It's mine."

I kept reading as the pages described Ordinary's battle with the Dream Giver. Then I found, scrawled in a script different than anything else he had written, his last entry in his journal.

I am surrendering my Dream to you, Dream Giver. I've decided that it is you that I can't go on without. [2]

I sat for a moment staring at those words. A dream without the Dream Giver meant nothing. It's not the dream that made this such important work. It was the God who gave me the dream and the skills and the platform. If God is asking for those things now, I don't want to keep them. It wasn't long after that I fell back on the bed, arms relaxed, hands open.

MY RESPONSE: I LET GO of a dream that was never really mine. I lifted my open hands, with everything I valued in them; my girls, Rennie, my church, my role at church, my gifts. I surrendered it all. I will do as He asked. I will give him back the dream.

****

It was November before I felt I could finally finish my work at the church! I had volunteered in a local church most of my life. For the last few months, I was finally getting paid for what I had trained all my life to do. Now I was letting go of the dream. I had to focus on my own health, our family, and my sweet girls.

Together, Christy and I decided our last Sunday would be a celebration. We hosted a service called ***Evidence of Grace,*** using a worship musical tracing God's hand of grace written by Steve Moore and David T. Clydesdale.[3]

We included testimonials of individuals and families from our church, mixed in with songs of triumph and humble confessions. My heart was filled with gratitude, as stories from within our church family pointed over and over to God's grace at work in their lives.

There was Merv and Laura, the couple who had lost their young son several years earlier. They shared their story for the first time.

There was the brother and sister who had lost their mom to ALS not long before. John Mark sang the words to "*I Can Only Imagine*" and his sister, Meghan, dressed in white, danced to express that meaning beautifully.

There were the young people who joined voices to challenge the congregation to *"Say it loud, say it strong. Tell the world what God has done!"* Youth were challenging their elders. Don't be quiet about what God is doing! Tell the world!

Also, it was one of the last times that our family joined our voices to a Philips, Craig and Dean song, *"Your Grace Still Amazes Me"*.[4]

I started by singing on the 1st verse.
>   *My faithful Father, enduring Friend*
>   *Your tender mercy's like a river with no end*

Then Ren's voice took the lead.
>   *It overwhelms me, covers my sin*
>   *Each time I come into Your presence*
>   *I stand in wonder once again*

As the music continued to play, each of us spoke a part of our family story.

>   Leisha: This past year hasn't exactly been one we would have chosen.

>   Rennie: All of our lives, we have sought to follow God. But now more than ever we were forced to trust in the darkness, what we had believed about God in the light.

>   Brie: And it was in these times of struggling we realized we didn't have to wait for God's grace.

>   Kathy: We found it right where we were!

>   Brie: So even when Mom was so weak she couldn't stand...

>   Leisha: Or the kitchen was completely torn out and remodeled--quite unexpectedly. *(That's a story I haven't even shared here!)*

Cait: Or we spent two months separated while Brie went through an intense treatment center...

Ren: We learned the real grace was never in the good times or bad--it was in the peace that came from knowing our Lord.

The girls united on the 2nd verse
What can I give You, Lord, what can I say
I know there's no way to repay You
Only to offer You my praise

We all joined together with the choir on the chorus
Your grace still amazes me
Your love is still a mystery
Each day I fall on my knees
'Cause Your grace still amazes me

It's deeper, it's wider, It's stronger, it's higher
It's deeper, it's wider, It's stronger, it's higher
than anything my eyes can see

'Cause Your grace still amazes me[4]

Yes! That told our story! His grace did amaze us. If it were not for his grace, we would not be here together as family to give testimony. None of these stories would be shared! And they needed to be shared. We all needed to remember his work happening right before our eyes.

The service ended. I knew I had done, maybe for the last time, what I was made to do. I had no dream now. I didn't know what came next.

And that was ok!

MY RESPONSE: I LET GO of a job that was never really mine. I did what I could--and walked away! Heart at peace! Hands Open!

****

I spent the next year pondering what God was doing in this process. I wasn't complaining! In fact, I was quite ok with it! I felt my body gaining strength. I watched the girls engage in our times together, and I felt at peace.

At Peace until...Ren began *letting go* of his dream too!

LORD! It was one thing for me to let go of my best dream, as long as Rennie was still a pastor. Alongside my best dream had always been another dream to be a pastor's wife. For most of my life, that's all I wanted to be.

I remembered our 3rd date, when I asked Ren what he wanted to be when he grew up. "A pastor!" he said. And I said I wanted to be a pastor's wife! These had been life-long passions for us. I thought I could never let go of mine. But I did!

Now this? Nearly 30 years later, he is considering not being a pastor anymore. It was September, 2005, nearly a year after I had "given back a dream".

Rennie was walking away, not only from the church we had served for 13 years, but from ministry as we had known it for the past 20 years. Now Ren was left to wrestle with how to provide for our family, but he was also struggling with his identity now that he wasn't a pastor. What do you do when everything you have ever studied for, or all you have ever worked for was to be a pastor able to serve a local church?

In his desperation, he became pretty creative. Ren worked very hard to generate an income for our family through a small business he created called "All Things New!" It is an automotive appearance repair business, and he has done a great job with it.

However the more he worked on his business, the more I resisted it. The more help he needed, the more busy I became in outside things, so I didn't have to help!

This is where the TRUTH blasted me once again.

You see, one morning I woke from a dream, rather it was a very vivid vision. It made me keenly aware that I wanted Rennie to fail at this job. I wanted the business to flop, so we could get back to what I wanted to be about--being a pastor's wife. That's the plain and simple of it. I hesitate to share this part of my journey here. But there it is! That's the ugly truth of it. I had put on my spoiled little girl shoes, dug in my heels, and waited for the day I could get what I wanted.

It is a sad thing to realize I had built a large part of my identity on something someone else had to do. And now, no matter how badly I wanted that identity back--or how hard I tried--I couldn't MAKE it happen! You can't be a pastor's wife when your husband is no longer a pastor.

Ugh! Rennie, I'm so sorry!

So now what? Lord, what does this mean? Why did you ask both of us to give back the dream? I don't get it!

But I am certain of this.

For the time being, God is growing in Rennie a new dream. It's not just about cars, but about the people he works with and for at the shop. It includes ministry. It is just different than before.

And God is growing a new dream in me; one that allows me to be me, doing many of the same things I did before, just in a different role. After all, it was never about the role and always about being who God made me to be in it. I can do that in any role.

More importantly, I am Rennie's wife! I love him very much. I want to partner with him in whatever God plants in our hearts to do for as long as God wills and I am able. No matter if it is as an auto appearance repair man's wife or something else!

I am Rennie's wife! I love you Ren!

What's next, Lord?

MY RESPONSE: I LET GO of a title that was never really mine. I took off my 'spoiled little girl' shoes and came alongside my husband. We're in this together!

10 Healing Summer of '06

Even though the year that followed was extremely difficult, the year of 2006 was a year of learning to dance. It was a dance of healing for us all. Remember, in Chapter 8, I used a quote by Jerry Sittser from *A Grace Disguised*,

> *It is not...LOSS that becomes the defining moment of our lives,....! It is HOW WE RESPOND to loss that matters.*[1]

I had focused on that part of the paragraph pretty intensely during the previous year. But it wasn't until I had some free quiet time that summer of 2006 that I dared to consider how Sittser continued that thought.

> *It is how we respond to loss that matters... That response will largely **determine** the quality, the direction, and the impact of our lives.... This book is intended to show how it is possible to **live in** and be **enlarged by loss**, even as we **continue to experience it.**"*[2] (**Bold Italics** are my own.)

I took out my life map and begin to pencil in all I had seen in 2006. I was conscious that I felt it was a GOOD year; as Jerry said, it was "enlarging"!

- Ren began his new business called "All Things New".
- We found a new church to 'hide' in, even if we weren't ready to invest ourselves in another place right now.

Well, Ren and I hid. Leisha thrived on the worship team and as a student leader in the Jr High youth.

- Ren began to find purpose with his business and began to laugh again.
- I began to hum again and felt much better!
- The girls noticed and responded and were doing their own laughing and humming.
- The five of us even took a ballroom dance class with two other families.

Our relationships were growing to new depths as we felt our family being resurrected. We were getting a second chance. That summer we spent some great quality time with extended family; dancing with cousins getting married, celebrating with grandparents after 50 years of marriage.

Each event allowed us to touch base with most of the extended family that summer which proved to be such a gift! Each of us began to feel more hopeful and more settled. I felt like this new place demanded another change, a change of a name.

Renaming the girls

While we had carefully chosen the names we had given the girls at birth, through our counseling, we began to realize that our words and responses to the girls had in many ways given them new names. Some were good, but others not so much. Being interested in people and their behaviors anyway, I watched with great curiosity as the girls were growing up.

I often recall one summer day at the county fair. The girls were quite young; Leisha may have been 3 or 4. We walked the fairway and found a ride that looked fun for all of them. It was a small child's version of a roller coaster train. As we waited for our turn, I observed each girl's expression. Cait kept asking us questions feeling very responsible for the girls since we would not be able to ride along. Brie was jumping up and down with excitement. Leisha kept curiously trying to see how this thing worked and if she could get closer to those tracks.

As they boarded their little train car, their demeanors never wavered. Cait scurried around making sure each of the girls were belted in and safe before she herself sat down and buckled up. Brie just bounced in her seat, hands on the bar in front of her, ready for action. Leisha had climbed out of her seat belt and was leaning over the car to see what the wheels looked like on the track. Cait had just seen this and was working to unbuckle her own seat belt again to pull Leisha back when the man running the ride came to the rescue. With all three finally seated and buckled, off they went.

That day, I named them responsible, excited and curious.

Over the years, other names might have been

Reader
Artist
Debater
Musician
Pastor's daughter
Beautiful
Creative
Organizer
Arranger

But as much as I love my girls, somewhere along the line they took on names like:

One who hides
Fearful
Ashamed
Guilty
Out of control

In the way
Assistant to Mom or Co-worker with Dad, and that wasn't a good thing

As we continued counseling as a family, and became increasingly aware of the names they owned, I knew I wanted to be part of renaming them. In biblical times, the Hebrew people would often receive new names:

Abram to Abraham, Genesis 17:5
Sarai to Sarah, Genesis 17:15
Jacob became Israel, Genesis 35:10

These are just 3 examples from the Old Testament, and each time, the new name was given in connection with a blessing and a promise from God.

I wanted to give them names of blessing; names that spoke life, not despair. It was Christmas, 2004, and my gift to each of them was a necklace with a ring on it that contained a single word. I had a necklace with all three rings on it.

- To Caitlin, I gave the word STRENGTH.
- To Brielle, I gave the word SPIRIT.
- To Leisha, I gave the word COURAGE.

I saw each characteristic in each girl so clearly with these words.

Cait was strong, physically strong yes, but more than that she had strength of mind and of heart. She could observe aspects of life to make things flow better. Structure and order that she suggested made our lives stronger as she tweaked the way we did things.

Brie was spirit, flitting here and there, adding sparkle and energy to a group. She could perceive what people were saying and help them see it too. Art and design gave dimension and texture to our hearts as we lived around her.

Leisha was courageous. It showed up in the way she pursued life. She saw a need and responded. She heard a challenge and stepped up to it. Inside I know she felt afraid, but it didn't keep her from trying something or speaking to someone.

I know this meant a lot to the girls, because they have often spoken of these words. But my heart ached as I read Leisha's journal entry about it.

My fears that I cannot release stay close with a steadfast reach
I hold them close for fear of discovery in my world of pain and agony.
I would like to say I can release them to God
But they are my safety,
My world of pain
This is my security as sad as it is
I am weary and sick as this war I fight
Becomes tedious and frustrating.
No one will listen, no one will understand.
No one, no one at all.
God is here though I cannot feel or understand him
I have to rely on what I know
And that will give me a safety net.
Freedom seems a faded dream
I want to go to my family and show them my world
But they will not listen or understand.
Long ago I would have told all to them
But I don't want them to pry me with questions
That I haven't the heart to answer.
Sad things fill my mind as I sleep.
It makes me feel guilt and shame that I feel as I do.
But I have to be honest here
Here in the silence where no one will see.
I fear everything
And mom gives me the ring of courage.
In my mind I am honored, but in my heart

I wonder why she gives it to me.
I am searching for freedom
Security
A safe place
The strength to be <u>REAL!</u>

Allender writes, *"Our families name us without knowing the consequences. So our life is a journey to discover our true name, though sadly, many of us never choose to begin the search."*[3] *(To Be Told, pg 34)*

Leisha had begun to search! Many of us never get around to searching for our name. It is hard work, and we must faithfully listen for it. It is also risky.
- What if we miss hearing it?
- Or we fear what it might actually be?
- Or what if we hear it, but those closest to us negate what we've heard.

Leisha wanted to know her true name and she wanted it to be good! With tremendous courage, Leisha had begun her search for the courage to be REAL! We had all come so far--but in the end, it is a dance we must each learn alone; the dance to our true name.

****

Our family was invited to join two other families for a ballroom dance class during July and August of that summer. Between the three couples we had enough boys to partner with girls. Every Friday night we gathered to practice our skills on the new step being taught to us. We tried the fox trot, the cha-cha and, of course, the waltz. We had even started to learn swing, which I think might have been my favorite.

Even though Rennie was working hard to master each step, I

found it difficult to pay attention. It was fascinating to watch each couple tackle each dance step, especially since these young couples were friends, but not dating. I could tell so much about the relationships as I watched.

Some were focusing on the task at hand and managing quite well. Others were quite interested in the relationship and that seemed to mess up their performance a bit. As for the three married couples, our time on the dance floor spoke volumes about how we danced off the dance floor in our married life.

- Who's leading anyway?
- How do I know what you are going to do next?
- How can we partner so we move together?

The people-watching was fascinating! I leaned in to Rennie at one point and said, "We need to incorporate this into any marriage counseling we do from now on." It only briefly occurred to me that we had not done any counseling, pre-marital or otherwise, since he wasn't a pastor anymore.

****

Summer was about to end. Our last dance lesson would be next Friday. Today was Sunday.

Journal entry:
August 13, 2006

There's been a releasing in life lately.
A releasing:
A Dance class:
I never 'danced'--couldn't
I was a preacher's kid remember (chapter 1),
but I loved to dance.

Dream:
I said "no" to a dream I never dreamed I would,
but I am beginning to dream again;
a new dream, with a new song!

We are
Laughing more
Singing more
Dancing more
Spending time with Ren more
Cleaning and uncluttering more
Experiencing more at church
Knowing more people

But alongside that is a frustration:
Learning to dance--with no place to dance
Having a passion for the local church--
but not really landed in one
Recognizing the majesty of God-—
but sensing I don't want to know the just side of God.

What am I feeling?
Is it discontent?
What does it mean?
Where do we fit?
What are we to do?
What's next?
Can't you do something?

Lord, you've led me to Revelation!
In it I read You are the Alpha and Omega
The Beginning and the End
The First and the Last
You are the one who is
Who always was
Who is still to come
The Almighty One
The Living One who Died!

Continue to teach me about you, Lord!
Three days later Leisha died.

AND THEN SHE DIED

11 August 16, 2006

The day started. as many summer mornings had. with the girls leaving early for work. All three of them had spent the summer working for Suter's Farm Produce which required they be in the cornfields picking corn by 5:30am. They rarely complained. Working with Jerry Suter was physical work; picking corn, filling bags, tying bags, loading trucks. Each job had a name: pickers, fillers, and tiers, or something like that!

Jerry had a way of connecting with the kids--40-80 of them in a season. They laughed, sang songs, told stories and attentively listened to the stories Jerry would tell. All the while they were working hard to get the work done. Best boss they ever had! That's what the girls still call Jerry to this day.

As each team came in from the fields and the trucks were loaded, Jerry would gather the whole gang together for Team Time. For the next 10-15 minutes, Jerry or someone he invited to share (which could be a worker or a guest) gave a challenge or encouragement to the kids. All of them huddled around, standing under the big tree in the yard, or sitting on the back of the produce trucks.

The girls would often come home and tell stories of the happenings that day, something Jerry did or something that was shared at Team Time. I was always so grateful for Jerry and

Nancy and the work they did in the fertile life of a kid, not just the rich farmland that produced their livelihood.

Today only Brie and Leisha went to the farm. Cait had not been feeling well so she stayed home. Both girls got home about 8am, showered, dressed, and pushed me out the door. I was the slow one. We were leaving early to get to an appointment with the girls' therapist. The drive was about an hour and we would just make it.

Brie drove. Leisha rode shotgun! They listened to music and talked all the way. I sat in the back marveling at the fun they had. Leisha fell asleep shortly before we arrived at the counselor's office. She was a bit of a grump when she woke up, so Brielle had gone in first. By the time she was done, Leisha was back to her normal, witty self.

After their sessions, we treated ourselves to lunch at Steak n Shake. Leisha was being goofy--talking, not eating. She shared all kinds of dreams she had for her future.

> Dream of being the debate champion of the debate tournament this next season.
> Dream of being the concertmaster (1st chair violin) in the Youth Symphony she played in.
> Dream of being one of the youngest Mary Kay Directors so she could pay her way through college.

So many dreams!

Brie was rapping her fingernails against the table by now, getting impatient that Leisha wasn't eating fast enough. But she graciously contributed to the lunch bill anyway.

What was supposed to be a quick trip to Walmart proved to have its own challenges. The girls dropped me off at the door and went to park the van. I went in to get milk, but when the girls caught up with me, my cart had fruits and vegetables, but no milk. They took off to the back of the store mumbling something about me not getting done what we came here to do. Cait called to check up on us, but I hung up quickly when I saw the girls sliding down the wide open aisles, each carrying a couple of gallons of milk. I was glad there weren't many people there that time of day.

Leisha was in front, but Brie yelled at her to help with something. Leisha turned around just in time to see Brie toss a carton of sour cream to her. She set her milk down quickly, but not quick enough to catch the carton. Sour cream hit the floor and splattered over and up Leisha's legs. A squeal came from both girls, laughing yet concerned what my reaction would be. I had to laugh looking at the expression on their faces, but I kept a straight face in the moment and firmly said, "Ok girls! Find a way to clean it up!"

The whole drive home, I watched them and wondered how I was going to manage this year with just the two of them. Cait would head off to college next week, Brie would start her senior year, and Leisha would be a sophomore. I wanted to enjoy this year. Time was precious and they were growing so fast, but sometimes I just felt like I was pulling out all my hair in the process. They did know how to push all my buttons.

As we brought in the groceries and started to put them away, I heard Leisha whisper loudly enough for me to hear, "Do you think Mom noticed one of the gallons of milk is brown?" She winked at her sister. I turned away smiling to myself. I was surprised only one was chocolate!

****

Brielle took off right away for a friend's house; it was too nice of a day not to be by a pond. Cait was upstairs, feeling some better, but not great yet. I was doing some Mary Kay work, filling orders for my clients.

Leisha was antsy. "Gotta go! Gotta go! Gotta go right now!" kind of antsy! She kept coming up with plans.

Mom, let's go early to Bible Study and get a cup of coffee first! Mom, let's go out to eat! (We had just forced her to eat some of her meal at Steak and Shake for lunch.) Mom, let's go for a drive.

I didn't want to put her off! I knew the only reason she was asking me was I was her ride and her sisters already were occupied. But I needed a half hour to finish up some things.

In a minute, she came ready to go for a walk, headphones and phone in hand. As she left, I promised I would call her to find out where she was and we'd go to church.

A few minutes later she called quite excited. "Mom, I talked to Joanna, but she can't go--but Abby called and she is coming to get me. We're going out for coffee. Is that OK? I'm just gonna chill with her tonight and skip youth group. OK Mom?"

I smiled. She had a plan.

She quickly told me she was just past Mr. B's house. She wondered if she could just keep walking to where she would meet Abby, and if I would be willing to bring her wallet and a glass of water. With lots of ice!

In earlier days, I probably would have insisted she go to youth group. She had made a commitment to them. But since we had been in counseling, and left ministry ourselves, I didn't want to use church as an obligation. I wanted her to want to go.

I asked her why she couldn't just come on home. She was less than a mile away. "Mom, Please! It's such a nice day, and Abby is going to meet me on the road."

"Ok, I'll come!" feeling a bit guilty that I hadn't taken her for coffee myself.

I got a mason jar with a handle on it and filled it with ice and water. I found her billfold and went to find her. I had every intention of picking her up and having that time with her that I put off earlier. I regretted not jumping at the chance. Now someone else would get her time.

I met her between the Diller's and Schumacher's. I just drove alongside her while she walked for a bit. But then I stopped in the middle of my lane. She came over and propped her arms in my van window and just started talking.

It was a breathtakingly, beautiful afternoon. I sensed then these were glorious minutes. The sun gave her beautiful brown hair (*a new color for her*) a glorious radiance. Her face was flush with the exercise, and her mind was full of thoughts. What was! What if! Could we? Random, yet ordered thoughts of what was and what could be; what she had learned and what she wanted yet to learn. I relished the moments as I watched the sparkle in her eyes flit from one thing to another.

I was teasing her about her impatience to turn 15 ½ and get her driver's permit. I jokingly said, "You just want power!" She paused, but I could see the wheels turning in her head. Then thoughtfully said words I'll never forget! "Mom, I don't want power. I want to influence. I want to be able to say, I'm going-- come with me!"

I replied to her, as I stroked her nose like I had done so many times since the day she was born, "Honey, you were made to influence!"

I tried one more time to snatch her up for my own coffee time with her, but she was eager to meet Abby. I drove away thanking God for the way he had created her and grateful for her passion to impact people for him.

Five minutes later, as I dropped my keys on the kitchen counter and started through the mail, a neighbor called. "Kathy, Leisha has been hit by a car! Can you come?"

Five minutes from where we spoke.

Cait and I rushed to her, but she was gone!

Leisha had walked the rest of the mile. Her friend, Abby, had driven up to the intersection just as Leisha got there! Abby honked her horn to let Leisha know it was her. Leisha looked up--squealed with delight--and ran without looking, into the path of a car.

She had been killed instantly.

All I could say was "O!" It wasn't a word. It was just a sound from the core of my being.

****

Memories blur from that point. Random images still appear in my mind at the most unexpected times.

There is the scene of a police officer standing by the side of the road near my daughter's body.

There was Abby on her knees a short distance away sobbing with

3 girls standing nearby.

There was Cait, who had jumped out of the van as we drove up to run to where Leisha was followed by her blood-curdling scream.

It was then that I walked as if in a fog to Leisha, her bloodied body lying in a shallow ditch. Even as I witnessed the scene, I screamed at the young officer, "Why don't you do something?" but I could not bend down to do it myself. Another man came to drag me away. He invited me to call my husband. I couldn't remember where my phone was.

Cait ran over to me, not as hysterical, but saying over and over, "I love you Mom! I love you so much! I'm not going back. Mom, don't make me go back?" For some reason, I thought she meant she wasn't going back to college next week. It was years later when I realized she meant not going back to where Leisha was. Funny what the brain does in times like that.

Cait handed me my phone. I tried to call Ren, but couldn't seem to dial the number. Each time I tried I hit a wrong number. I must have dialed 14 times. I finally handed it to the man next to me and said, "Please, just dial it for me!'

When Ren answered all I could say was, "Honey, hurry! It's not good. They are not doing anything. They won't let me near her."

WHY? Why isn't someone helping Leisha! WHY!!!! "O"

A neighbor woman stepped up to me. "Kathy, I checked for pulse immediately after it happened. I found nothing. She was gone instantly."

No! How could this be! She was just fine--glorious in fact, full of life and vitality! How could she be gone just like that! What happened?

A few minutes later, neighbor friends Tammy and Diane were holding my arms praying for a miracle. I knew they were not just praying but holding me up. EMT's came. I watched as they held up sheets and began to work on her! We prayed!

Of course! They will work on her and she will be revived. God I know you can do that! She will be a miracle!

He didn't! They didn't! She didn't!

WHY?? "Oh God! O"

I called over to Marv's house where Brie was, but I don't remember talking to them. I think someone else took the phone.

I told the EMT that I had Addison's Disease. That means I can't handle stress! How does any mother handle this kind of stress? I had a syringe in my purse I carry for emergencies. I never dreamed I would have one like this. Cait kept trying to get the right stuff out of my purse. It was always the wrong thing. She brought it to me so I could find it myself.

Joe and Joyce were there! Then Jerry came! All are part of the Suter family. Leisha died on the corner of the Suter farm where she had loved to work. Jerry hugged me hardest! I looked at him--a father who had lost his own son a few years earlier. He hugged me, then stumbled over to the other side of the road and fell down on the grass in sobs.

Oh God! Jerry knows something I don't know yet!

Where is Rennie?

Then I saw Christy, my best friend and Abby's mom! We had

shared a lot of life, and here we were bonded by another event we would never have asked for. I saw her bound out of the car, frantic to find her daughter Abby. I grieved for Abby. She sat cross-legged, head hung over, numb and wailing in agony when I first saw her. Now she finally cried in her mom's arms. I died for her over what she must have witnessed.

I tried to sit with Christy and her husband, Steve, for a while. But I couldn't sit still. Partly the circumstances, partly the meds I had been given. Adrenalin was flowing. and I had to be moving.

So many people began to arrive, so many standing by! Most of them I knew from our former church, from the community, friends of the girls. Geoff and Pam came! My first thought was she looks good! She had gone through her own pain but was looking better. Yet the pain on their faces foretold what was yet to come.

I kept watching for Brie to arrive! Then I saw Marv's van come down the road and park in the long line of cars gathering. Brie came flying toward me in her little gray sundress. "Where is she, Mom? I've got to see her, where is Leisha? Tell me where she is!"

I held her face in my hands, trying to get her to calm down and focus--words racing through my head how to best say such awful words.

She's gone, Brie!

Instantly her legs began to give way. Her words short and emphatic! "NO! NO! I HATE GOD! I HATE GOD!" The Sheriff was by our side instantly, Cait grabbed us from the other side. As she fell to the ground, I felt my thumbnail bend back. I remember looking at it and straightening it, recognizing that it didn't hurt a bit. I was numb!

I tried to get Brie off the rough cornfield ground. She was writhing, her little heart trying to absorb what I had just said. The Sheriff lifted her up.

Then suddenly she calmed--the three of us were clutching each other. With a nearly lifeless expression, Brielle looked up at me. "Oh Mom! Are you OK? I love you! I love you so much. Oh Mom!" We three held each other!

More people! So many! They hugged me, hugged each other! Leisha had been a year old when we moved to this place. They had watched her grow up and play soccer and debate. Some adopted us as family and had come to her concerts or the local basketball games.These weren't just tears for us! They were weeping out of their own grief.

From a mile away, I saw Ren's silver van turn the corner to come toward us.I began to walk down the middle of the road. Neighbors surrounded me, but I said "No! I have to go to him alone." As he slid out of the van, all I could say was "Honey, she's gone!"

He stepped toward me and we embraced, suddenly surrounded by a swarm of people holding us. I felt Ren 'flip the switch'. "Ok, what do we have to do?"

"Oh God"

We spent the next few minutes answering questions for the authorities; her address, social security, birthdate. There were so many different questions. We lamented with the next person who came. We watched as the EMT's did more at the scene. Then Ren said, "I want to see my girl!" He clasped my hand but I pulled back. I couldn't go. Not now. I watched as he disappeared under the tent, and I visualized him as he knelt down beside her.

I wept.

As they lifted her body into the ambulance, they invited Ren and me to go to her again. This time I needed to be with her one last time.

As I stepped through the doorway, I was struck instantly! She was not there! Her body lay there, but her face was completely void of color--lips blue, face white. Her hair-- vibrant with color just moments ago--was matted with her blood. There were scrapes on the left side of her face, but the other was perfectly smooth. The EMT sat at her head and held the towel on her left side.

She had left us. She was not in this body. Her spirit--all that was full of life when I last spoke to her--was gone! It was a major contrast to my precious 10 minutes with her just yards away from where she was found.

I stroked her nose, kissed her cheek, wept with her father. Then Ren left to get her sisters. The holiness of the moment was so vivid to me! Here I sit alone, except for the EMT seated near her head. I was so aware of death--yet so full of a peace that I had never known. She was safe! She found a Narnia Door and was caught up into the Lord's presence in a breath. I marveled at the sensation of the moment.

After a few minutes, I found myself uneasy being alone, so I peered out the door. I saw them come--Ren, with a daughter on either side. They were so unsure yet holding tightly to their father's arms. I wept for what they were about to do. Many who stood nearby prayed.

The girls came to the door but hesitated to enter. They wept. Ren gathered us up, and we joined hands; I holding Leisha, and each of them holding me. We prayed.

"We're giving her back to you, Lord! Not willingly--we have no choice. So we release her to You!"

"O God!"

Brie stepped in to stroke her nose too! Cait reached in to brush her cheek. We cried! The EMT cried too!

We stepped out; all eyes were on us even though it was beginning to get dark. Nothing will ever be the same--not without Leisha! She had run on before us right into Glory!

"O God!"

It was on the drive home I began to hum a tune! I wasn't really paying attention to it until we sat in silence on the ride home. There it was! The words became clear as the melody continued:

I hear
Leisha
Singing in heaven tonight!
I hear
Leisha
Telling me that she's alright. [1]

Tears ran down my cheeks as I recalled the musical that had inspired her name.

"O God! It's happening again!"

Journal Entry:
One of those days! (Aug 16, 2013)

Ever have a day that you can remember almost every detail of?

This date is one of those days for me! August 16, 2006

I remember waking up with an agenda
I remember the car ride, tired eyes and silence, laughter and talking.
I remember conversations and laughter over shakes at *Steak and Shake*.
I remember a sour cream carton being pitched across the aisle only to come crashing to the floor
and more laughter and some clean up.
I remember wondering how I was going to make it without getting upset.
I remember wanting to laugh but feeling like I had to be responsible.
I remember dreams and plans being made.
I remember saying "no" when I should have said "yes"
and saying "yes" when I could have said "no".
I remember sparkling eyes, flush face, and fresh hair color and more dreams being shared.
I remember last words.
I remember caring arms, and tears shed and disbelief.
I remember hearing the scream.
I remember a father falling to the ground in tears.
I remember meeting a new face--one I will pray for forever.
I remember numbness, yet feeling fully alive!

Completely aware of so many thoughts and emotions and sensations.
Only beginning to realize that God must be bigger than I had ever known him to be
for this to be good
or for me to survive.
I remember humming her song on the way home
only to burst into tears when I recalled the words.
I remember not being able to imagine I could sleep-
only to wake to a morning sky
 the sun still long from shining bright, but already making her presence known.

Days like that happen only a few times in our lives.

Some things I will forever hold precious
Others bring sharp pain and often a gasp
Still others deep, deep gratitude and soft, gentle tears.

No, days like that are one of a kind!
I never want to forget this day!

I love you, Leisha!

12 Tracing Leisha

Leisha was only 15. She was bold, courageous, and full of vitality. We remember the way she quoted movie lines at just the right moment or said what the rest of us were thinking at what might have seemed the worst moment. She played violin in the area youth symphony, keyboard on the church worship team, and basketball with the homeschool team.

She loved words--anything to do with words: debating, singing, journaling, talking, emailing, etc. One of her greatest joys was being a student leader for the Jr High group at church. Her friends considered her a best friend; her teachers and employers thought her a favorite. She was described as a cross between Miss America and the President of the United States. That's our Leisha.

One of the quotes she referred to over and over again was,

> *"Go after God. Whatever it takes, do it. And don't give the excuse, 'I am just a teenager; or 'I'll do that when I grow up,' because it doesn't work that way. God wants to know you NOW!"*[1]

The quote was taken from the pages of *"The Journals of Rachel Scott, a Real Diary of Faith"*. Rachel had been killed in the shootings at Columbine High School at the age of 17 on April 20, 1999. Her book had inspired Leisha to begin her own journal.

Today I'm so grateful to have her thoughts in writing and on her tape journals. How precious they are!

Losing a loved one so unexpectedly means there is no time to prepare. One moment she was vibrant, full of life and sparkle. The next moment she lay void of any and all life. I'm not saying it is easier losing a loved one after a long battle with cancer. Not at all! Death or illness or other losses can be devastating no matter how it comes.

It would be untrue to say my life flat-lined the day Leisha died. It didn't! In fact, for a couple of weeks, we were so surrounded by people we loved, I was coping quite well. The shock to my system was quite effective at numbing the reality that I had lost a child. It wasn't that I didn't acknowledge Leisha was gone; it was that I didn't OWN it. My feelings and emotions weren't lining up with the facts.

However, even the night of her accident, I found myself asking one question.

Why would God allow this?

He knew he had created her to influence. I wasn't the only one to know it. I had often been told by others in her world that she was bold with her faith, impacting in her relationships, and sold out to the God who made her. This surely wasn't part of the "all the days ordained for her"! Or for me!

It prompted me to find the text she had been working on so intently. She wouldn't let me read it until she had the wording just right. Then, with some ceremony just a few weeks before her accident, she presented it to me to ponder.

> *I chose to be in the world though not of it when I chose to follow you, trial I knew would push me far from you, but I am running still as you ask me to.*

I crawl through the mud for my legs can go no further.
You pick me up and carry me as a child in your arms,
you take me to a place of safety,
a place of hope,
a place of beauty and joy
a place known to me only in story books and fairy tales.
You take me home.

My porcelain heart seems to break at every turn
but hope I see is not far from me,
for you open the skies to rain down your mercy
and then bring sweet rays of sunshine upon my face.

So heal me now, Lord,
for you are the potter, I am the clay.
God, I now say the words I fear most.
I surrender.

With eerie accuracy, I could almost hear her read these words to me now; Lord, *You pick me up and carry me as a child in your arms, you take me to a place of safety, a place of hope, a place of beauty and joy...you take me home.*

What had God done to prepare her to write these words? Were they for her? Or for me? Or for him?

Her last paragraph spoke to my *porcelain heart that seems to break at every turn*, **but hope I see is not far from me**... *heal me now!*, **I surrender!**

I pondered those last two words often, each day becoming more aware of the fear involved in surrender. I thought I knew what she meant that day after her death. But as time went on I discovered I was nowhere close to understanding.

It was the day after her memorial service when I finally sat down to read through her most recent journal. It was filled with random thoughts of her day and her life. I was pleased to see she had started a gratitude journal.

She had come to the kitchen a week earlier and had shared how discouraged she was about life and about relationships. I had encouraged her to find five things she was grateful for every day before she went to bed. She had told me the day before she died that she felt like the gratitude journal was working. Now I was grateful that I had made it on her gratitude list--a couple of times!

If you opened the journal from the other direction, it was her book.

Her title was "Lovely Traces". Then Chapter One! Once upon a time...!

She told the story of how her Dad and I met and married, where we lived, when her older sisters were born, and even the story of baby Eric and my struggle with God. Then she wrote...

"but Mom decided that she would trust God, and I was born. Leisha Danae Burrus, April 28, 1991."

Wow! Just 16 years earlier, I had arrogantly told God to *'take her'* thinking I had the *right* solution to a tragic situation with Baby Eric. But I had been **so grateful** every day since that he had not listened to me.

Now she was gone! And here in her own words, I heard the challenge that once again I must *trust God!* What would that mean this time?

Earlier that morning I had picked up my Bible to continue

reading where I had left off the day before. I was beginning the book of Revelation. As John, the author of the book, was *worshiping in the Spirit,* he writes,

> *¹⁰Suddenly, I heard behind me a loud voice like a trumpet blast. ¹¹ It said,* **"Write in a book everything you see, and send it** *to the seven churches ....* **¹²** *When I* **turned to see** *who was speaking to me, I saw seven gold lampstands.* **¹³** *And standing in the middle of the lampstands was* **someone like the Son of Man.** *He was wearing a long robe with a gold sash across his chest.* **¹⁴** *His head and his hair were white like wool, as white as snow. And his eyes were like flames of fire.* **¹⁵** *His feet were like polished bronze refined in a furnace, and his voice thundered like mighty ocean waves.* **¹⁶** *He held seven stars in his right hand, and a sharp two-edged sword came from his mouth. And his face was like the sun in all its brilliance.²*

(Words in bold were what stood off the page for me that day) Then I read these words...

> **¹⁷** *When I saw him, I fell at his feet as if I were dead. But he laid his right hand on me and said,* **"Don't be afraid! I am the First and the Last.**
> **¹⁸** *I am the* **living one. I died, but look—I am alive forever and ever!**
> *And* **I hold the keys of death and the grave.**
>
> **¹⁹** *"Write down what you have seen—both the*

things that are now happening and the things that will happen.²

That's the real story--in my life and yours! It's the story of The LIVING ONE who Died and how he shows up in our stories.

I had been reminded of that truth from the first words of the first song at Leisha's memorial service. The worship team that Leisha had been on the Sunday before led us. Michael Wise strummed his guitar and boldly proclaimed,

"You lived! You died! You said in three days you would rise. You did! You're alive!"³

On that day I had already seen such intimate ways God had shown up for us. But I knew that the LIVING ONE would have to show up bigger than I had ever known him to be in order for me to survive Leisha's death. Even as the numbness of shock was beginning to wear off, I sat down to write.

****

I don't remember which morning it was--they all blurred together for a while. All I know is the house was still full of friends who had made their beds on the floor of our living room the night before so they could be with Caitlin and Brielle. Now they were already talking and fumbling around for breakfast.

As I followed Rennie downstairs, still combing through my hair with my fingers, I began the hum again quite unexpectedly. *I hear...Leisha...singing in heaven tonight.*

As soon as I caught myself, I was instantly mad. I had sung the song many times while she was alive. I had always changed the words to something like,

I hear Leisha... singing a new song tonight.

She had known the original words, because I had told her the story of the Leesha from the musical. There were many times she would say as I tucked her into bed, "Mommy, sing me my song."

I had noticed myself singing it often in the hours since she had died. But today it made me furious.

I reached up and with my fist pounded the low part of the stair ceiling with all the strength I could muster.

"I can't hear her God! I can't hear her sing! What are you going to do about that?"

Defiant! Angry! Desperately I blasted my words at a God I wasn't sure had paid attention the moment my baby girl ran across the road. He let her die! He won't do anything about this either! I'm not sure I had the emotional clarity to give words to my emotions then. But as I think now about that moment, I feel it physically all over again.

I turned the corner of the stairs and entered the living room; my eyes were full of tears and my heart ready to scream. I swallowed it all when I saw how many kids still sat at our breakfast table.

"Mom, look what we found!" Cait was certain that I would be glad about it. I could tell by her countenance.

She pushed play on a little tape recorder. Leisha spoke. I was startled. I hear Leisha! I don't recall her words, but in just a few seconds she said, "I feel like singing a song!"

Tears gushed from my eyes and sobs threatened to choke me as her voice spilled into the room.

Let everything that breathes praise you.

The earth, the sky, the sea praise you.

Just as nature shows to us Your blessing

Soon I find my heart confessing.

My love is not my own, it all belongs to You

And after all You've done the least that I can do

Is live my life

In every part

Only to please my Father's heart?

Leisha paused in the song, but it was only long enough for the interlude I would play in between the chorus and the next verse.

Love is all you need to heal us

Flowing from the Heavens, Jesus.

And with one voice we'll sing together

And this will be our song forever. [4]

I slowly slid down in my chair. I had all but cursed God for having abandoned me in this painful place. But seconds after my blaring burst of anger, he showed up with her voice.

And her song!

It was a different song than I had been humming before. A song I had heard her sing many times while I played for her at home, and again just weeks before when she had sung it for the weekend worship services at our church.

Her voice! Her song!

The tears couldn't keep from falling now!

God showed up, and he brought Leisha's voice with him.

If he would meet me so intimately in that moment, I had to believe he would meet me in the next, and the next, and the next.

It was my poignant memory of 'hope'!

****

The tape that Cait had played for me that day was one of several that Leisha had made. We had purchased a small tape recorder for her at the suggestion of her counselor.

'You can't possibly listen to all the words Leisha needs to say. But she still needs to say them. Get her a recorder so she can speak as much as she wants and then she can listen to her thoughts. It will help her process all the emotions she is carrying with her."

We knew the counselor was right! Leisha insisted we go the next day to see what we could find. One small handheld recorder, check. Two cassette tapes, check. One happy girl! Check. Check.

I knew she was using it on a regular basis. I would frequently interrupt her "recording sessions" when I would come up to say good night. Sometimes she would share her thoughts with me that she had been recording.

But now I drank in her words like the air I breathe.

Some of it was a typical teenage girl's random thoughts about boys and makeup and friends and boys. I sometimes shook my head knowing she would not want anyone else listening to these thoughts.

Occasionally she would even say, "Now if you are listening to this, I must be dead, because if I'm not and I catch you--you will be dead!" Other times it was as if she was talking to us. "Brie, if you are listening to this..." or "Mom, I think you know what I mean..."

I laughed out loud then burst into tears as I took in what she had just said.

For days after the family left for school or work, I would sit at the kitchen table with her recorder and a cup of tea. I would listen to every word for as long as my emotions would let me.

I wept that I had not just sat to hear every word while she was first saying them. Why had I been too busy to just listen to each one? Why did life keep me from just soaking in every goofy, friendly, happy, sad, depressed, empowered, fascinating word out of her mouth?

On one of those days when my emotions would not line up with the sun shining outside, I flipped on Leisha's tape and listened as Leisha closed off several days reflecting on Psalm 28:7.

> *The Lord is my strength and my shield;*
> *   my heart trusts in him, and I am helped.*
> *My heart leaps for joy,*
> *   and I will give thanks to him in song.*[5]

The first night she talked about the Psalm her ramblings went something like this.

> *It's hard to give joy to God right now or*
> *to have your heart leaping when it's broken in a million*
> *pieces*
> *The Lord is my strength--yeah, like I have a lot of strength*

right now.
He may be my shield but a whole bunch of bugs and insects have gotten past my shield and they've all stung me at once. That's how it feels!

I don't mean to be critical, well, right now I do. I'm so fed up with all the things that are happening.

I know that God is working, but there is so much pain. Lord, whatever you are going to do--I hope you do it fast. I hope you come tomorrow.

But a day or two later, her voice led me in a Bible Study of the same Psalm as she said "*Let's pull it apart, shall we!*"

Strength and shield
I have been so grateful at how he has been my strength. He has just been there for me in so many ways.

With everything that has been going on, he has been protecting me. It feels insane. Life feels insane, but I feel like he's been my shield against so many things.

My heart trusts in him.
It has too! Before I found out Mom had Addison's, there was nothing else to do but trust in him.

At EQUIP (the SONLIFE youth conference she had attended that summer), God just told me to trust him. I couldn't do anything else. I felt God saying over and over, "I love you! I love you, Leisha." It was like God's arms were around me and he was saying, "Leisha, honey, you can't control this. You are still a baby, you are only 13."

And I am helped.
I am helped. It's true. He sent me Kelsey, Sarah Ginther,

Lisa Gratz, and Aunt Cyndy too. She sent me a note this week and said she is praying for us, *"I've been a pastor's kid too. I haven't been through what you have been through, but you are doing a good job. Keep on!"* That helped.

My heart leaps for joy!

That I will get to see Breezy again. I'm so amazed that she has the courage to do this, to go to Remuda Ranch. To be honest, I don't think I could have done that. I talked to Dad about it. He said, *"Leisha, God would have given you the strength."* Sometimes I feel like I should be the one to muster the strength first, but maybe not.

I will give thanks

I don't know how I thank him! I guess I need to work on that.

In song

I'm not sure I know really what they mean. Sing thanks to him, I guess. I like to sing. I need to go to bed now, but I don't want to turn this off. This is so cool.

I smiled as I listened. She was 13 when she recorded her little lessons, but she had just taught me much. Each day is filled with emotions of their own. One day I feel abandoned by God and blame him for not being there. The next day I see so clearly how God is at work and the people he is using to care for me.

Maybe I need to work on giving thanks and singing praise in my own journey now.

I was reminded of the words of the Krystal Myers song that had inspired the title of her book called "Lovely Traces".

The chorus spoke clearly of her heart's desire.

Lovely traces fall behind you
Turn around and you will see
Lovely traces to remind you
Everything that you've been through
What it took to get you to me. [6]

Whoa! Did it take all of these Lovely Traces of Leisha-- of her journey to hope-- to get me to a new place of trusting God in my own?

I wept to think of all things she left for me; lovely traces to remind me that everything we've been through is what it took to get me to see God for who he really is.

Lovely Traces-- Krystal Meyers

I was consumed
By a life that I made
Destined to crash
Beat up and bruised
By the flashbacks of my own past
I tried to hide away
'Til I heard you say

[Chorus:]
Lovely traces fall behind you
Turn around and you will see
Lovely traces to remind you
Everything that you've been through
What it took to get you to me

All my mistakes
Regrettable choices I'd like to forget
But somehow you make
All that I wasted useful again
I thought I fell from grace
But you can't erase

[Chorus:]
The lovely traces behind you
Turn around and you will see
Lovely traces to remind you
Everything that you've been through
What it took to get you to me

I lost my direction
'Cause I couldn't see
What a beautiful picture
You would complete in me

[Chorus:]
The lovely traces behind you
Turn around and you will see
Lovely traces to remind you
Everything that you've been through
What it took to get you to me

Used with permission[6]

GREEN MEANS HOPE!

Artwork by Brielle Burrus Augsburger
110 Days of Green   April 2008 [1]

13 Take Off Your Clothes

Barb sat across from me at the table at Panera over a cup of coffee. "*The first 12 chapters you write as if you are standing among us naked and unashamed.*" I almost blushed when Barb spoke, suddenly feeling very vulnerable.

She continued, "*But in this last part, it's as if you put your clothes on. You become something else, a teacher, a coach, someone who invests in the lives of others but not going deep, being personal, or sharing intimately.*"

I had been working on this manuscript for a while now. I shared my first draft with six women I trust with my life. The comments I got helped me know if I had communicated what I hoped. But Barb showed me what I was *or wasn't* saying. I had quit being transparent in telling my story and started to act as if I had figured out why this had happened to Leisha, to me.

Immediately I knew she was right.

Every story has a beginning, middle and an end.

> ACT 1: introduces the hero, or heroine, her back story and sets up the 'inciting incident' she must overcome.

> ACT 2: the heroine begins her journey and wrestles with what it is going to take to accomplish the task and be victorious.

Act 3: the heroine wins. She proves she has overcome, learned the lesson, and completed the quest.

I looked back over my manuscript. My ACT 1 was actually in four parts. I introduced my family and shared some of our back story. Each chapter and 'story within a story' led up to the 'inciting incident' of Leisha's death.

When I think back to all that is included in ACT 1, the memories are in full color. Yes, there were hard times, but they are surrounded by light in my recall of them. I can write about them in vivid detail because I can see the moments. I can describe what happened even now.

But as I began to rewrite this next part, I pondered what Barb meant when she said I "put on my clothes". Each time I tried to write these next chapters, I tried to prove that I had "learned the lesson". For the next 10 weeks I attempted to be more real about this painful time of my life.

It slowly dawned on me that I was trying to write ACT 3 as if the story was complete and lessons were learned without writing Act 2. I was determined that if I had to hurt this bad that I would learn all I needed to learn to help someone else. Maybe I could keep them from hurting as bad as I was hurting. I wanted to be enlightened so I could move on quickly. So I tried to skip Act 2 altogether and go right into Act 3.

But I can't skip Act 2. No one can! I can't tell the story of how I overcame the pain until I identify the pain. I can't resolve the problem without recognizing the problem and what it is going to take to overcome.

I was mad that I couldn't just say I was done, not just with the writing of this book, but with the journey. But I was also determined that I wouldn't let this book go to print without attempting to be real with myself, whether I shared it with you, the reader, or not. I had to be transparent enough to remember what really happened during that dark time. Not just for me but for you!

How can I let you think that I figured it out and moved on when I continue to wrestle with the ache and the longing I feel? How can I write as one with all the answers when I am filled with more questions from the core of my being?

I had to know! I had to 'take off my clothes' and acknowledge what the real story was during that time. What was my story in the darkness? So I just opened my hands and said, "*Lord, please help me remember the things I need to know. Teach me what it is I need to learn from it and what I need to share with others.*"

Looking back at the days, weeks, and months after Leisha's death, all I see is a dark palette, almost completely black. At first that was all I saw. Darkness! Up Close!

But as I leaned into the darkness, I began to see traces of light, as if suddenly on a dark night, the clouds parted and the stars began to shine through. When I pressed my eye into the tunnel of black and embraced the sliver of hope that was lighting my way, I began to see parts of my story more clearly. Things that happened, images I had seen, people who cared, and lessons I learned were all part of the grief and the growth of that moment.

All of it is shrouded in black even still in my memory. Yet as I pressed closer into the light, I began to see those moments when God broke into my world--or when he didn't; at least when he didn't show up in a way that I expected to see him.

But to tell you about what I experienced is a different matter.

We've all fallen and skinned our knees or bruised our hearts. Brene Brown says in her book *Rising Strong*, *"The scars are easier to talk about than they are to show with all the remembered feelings laid bare. Rarely do we see wounds that are in the process of healing. I'm not sure if it is because we feel too much shame to let anyone see a process so intimate as overcoming hurt or if it's because even when we muster the courage to share our still incomplete healing, people reflexively look away."*[1]

Yes! That I could identify! There is a great vulnerability and yes, sometimes shame in the way I processed my grief. Her words resonated loud in my spirit as I read.

I wish I could say I did it all right. I wish I could say I always believed God to be the Blessed Controller of all things and therefore trusted him completely. But I didn't!

I wish I could say I had overcome my grief. But even now I have to ask, "Have I?"

It's true! There is this part of me that feels too much shame to let anyone see my process that was so intimate to me.

But I am also afraid if I muster up the courage to share what I know is still incomplete in me, will you dare to stay with me--to keep reading, to keep walking with me through this journey?

There are times when my friends have experienced a great loss and I sat with them in their moment of deepest grief as their pastor's wife, or coach or friend. There are times when their loss felt so painful I had to look away. I didn't want to look away. I tried not to. But I couldn't imagine what they were feeling. I didn't want to know that kind of pain.

We tend to prefer stories that have drama- some point of

intersection of pain with the leading character. But we always want that to end quickly and find a resolution so we can say, "Yeah, they overcame!" They made up, they kissed, they discovered the treasure, or they solved the mystery. They made it!

Brene writes, *"we like recovery stories to move quickly through the dark so we can get to the sweeping redemptive ending."*[2]

That is what I was doing. I tried to write ACT 3 without identifying how I got there. That is why I still struggle. I can't get there! Even now as I write, it has been almost 10 years since my daughter died. Yet I've spent these last couple of months back in a grief place. It is not what it once was--it is different now. But it is still a dark place; a place where I can't move, or think, or write. I can barely breathe.

I want to be at that *'sweeping redemptive ending'* and I'm not there.

I want to tell you my story in a way that tells you I made it! I want to shout God was enough; big enough, present enough, strong enough.

Yet I'm writing about a time in my life when I wasn't sure any of that was true. I didn't know if I could make it through this grief tunnel. I doubted if God was indeed who he said he was. That's not the kind of stuff you want to admit in a book called *Lovely Traces of Hope*. I didn't see it then. I sometimes struggle to remember it now.

But healing is a progression. Unless we embrace that dark tunnel, the loss or the failure, we can't acknowledge the traces of hope that help us deal with the real hurt and the fear that it can cause. We are just *'putting our clothes on'*, not in a sense to be modest but to remain hidden.

I put my clothes on because I didn't want to be that vulnerable with you. Yet even that is a lie. I didn't want to be vulnerable at all. I wanted to jump right to Act 3 with resolutions and answers instead of having to deal with the pain or the questions.

Act 2 is the time after Leisha died. There I see mostly darkness. That is how it looks in a tunnel--of mud--that swallows a person whole. That kind of heart break not only knocks the wind out of you, it leaves you unable to breathe. There is no light. There is no way to move.

Could I go through that place and ever feel life again?

Would I ever be able to let my daughters or my husband leave without fearing I might not see them again?

Would I be able to breathe again without having to tell myself to do it?

I spent a great deal of time wondering if I really wanted to go back there, to a place of feeling the pain again. It's not like I hadn't felt it the first time, but I hadn't let it do its work. I waved it away hoping not to feel it any more, or convey it had not changed me!

Only it had! It changed me! The pain and loss have made me different. But so did the love and the relationship with my daughter. To accept one aspect means I must respect the other and embrace the whole picture. It is a hard place, but it is good! My version of the story transformed!

I struggled with whether I could share ACT 2 with you, the reader. But to not go there means I didn't tell you the real story. And perhaps, if I find the courage to look into my darkness and find the traces of hope that show me the real story, you can too!

This isn't the first draft that Barb read. These next chapters tell of my incomplete journey to embrace the loss, the pain, the darkness. They speak to the questions that remain unanswered. They invite each of us to lean into all that is real to find lovely traces of faith, hope and love.

Lean in my friend! I need to tell you about Act 2.

14 Turning East

Grief is a lonely journey. We were a shell of a family left in a home that suddenly felt unsafe again. After all of our effort to restore our family, we were now separated by the darkness of our grief.

Actually we were three at home. We took Cait to college just days after Leisha's death. Sometimes I envied Caitlin's leaving, not having to live where we missed Leisha most. I am forever grateful for Cait's dear friends; Amy, Carmen, Arley and others who arranged for her to live in their dorm and reached out to her so much that year. But I also grieved for her to be two hours away from home.

We were all longing for home. Caitlin's trips home made us keenly aware of how home had changed and how intense our grief was. We were all surprised by the weight of it. We were living with it each day but her presence made us suddenly aware of how heavy grief had become.

There had been many times in our recent life as a family that we had fought to make a safe place in our home; allowing ourselves to be at peace with the mess in an effort to be real.

Leisha had reflected about some of the challenges we faced in one of her late night conversations with her tape recorder.

- She recalled the times I was sick and not able to be involved in the life of our family.

- She remembered the day we came home from a basketball tournament only to find our entire kitchen flooded from a burst pipe in the bathroom above it. As I lay on the sofa in the living room still undiagnosed, our carpenter buddies Marv and Greg tore out our kitchen and started over from scratch. The kitchen was the primary gathering place for us, yet it had represented a place of great unsafety as we dealt with the issues of disordered eating.

- She reflected on her emotions during the time that Brielle was at the eating disorder treatment center in Arizona.

As all these things were happening, home was not safe. In the privacy of her recorder, Leisha acknowledged she wanted to talk more about it with me, but was afraid it would *add to my tears!* While it saddened me to hear, I was grateful for people like Sarah G. and Lisa G. that had listened to her when she feared talking to me!

But now, Leisha was gone. Cait was at college.

Brie was desperately trying to get through her senior year; embracing what she could, furious that this special year was tainted with Leisha's absence. Her saving grace seemed to be her art teacher, "Mr. Will," who dismissed all the regular assignments and allowed her to express herself through paint. Most of her paintings had to do with Leisha. At first they were entirely black and white, but as the year went on she added color. Her last work was a triptych, a single piece of art painted over a series of 3 canvases. It was multi-colored in shades of green with a muted side portrait of Leisha blowing a dandelion puff. As the seeds break off and float away they become brightly colored butterflies, each one carrying the name of a friend or family member in its wings. But the journey to get to color--or to paint what she was acknowledging in her grief journey was long and deep. But that's a story for Brielle to tell.

Rennie and I were both filled with grief but displayed it so differently. Ren had no choice but to go back to work. He needed something to do with his hands, and our family needed him to continue to provide for us. He worked out many of his tears as he reshaped and made cars look like new. He wondered why he couldn't do that with his heart.

My only choice was to embrace the ache. I couldn't think outside of myself enough to do anything but allow my mother heart to grieve and try to do and be what my family needed right now.

Ren and I labored to care for one another. We were committed to each other, but longed for relief from our pain. To help the other became excruciating when we both carried such gaping, ripped holes in our own heart. Often all you can do is deal with your own stuff. It feels selfish, but grief is just a lonely journey, each of us trying to figure out how we can survive, and wondering if God would be big enough for us as we did.

On one of those days when the grief darkness threatened to overtake me, I read these words by Jerry Sittser; words that couldn't have described more accurately my own emotions if I had written them myself. So I'll let Jerry's words speak for themselves.

> *"I had a kind of waking dream...of a setting sun. I was frantically running west, trying desperately to catch it and remain in its fiery warmth and light. But I was losing the race. The sun was beating me to the horizon and was soon gone. I suddenly found myself in the twilight. Exhausted, I stopped running and glanced with foreboding over my shoulder to the east. I saw a vast darkness closing in on me. I was terrified by that*

darkness. *I wanted to keep running after the sun, though I knew that it was futile, for it had already proven itself faster than I was. So I lost all hope, collapsed to the ground, and fell into despair. I thought in that moment that I would live in darkness forever. I felt absolute terror in my soul."*[1]

Yes! That was what it looked like for me too! He got it! He described the chase in exact detail. I was urgently trying to make the day last because the night did indeed bring absolute terror!

Jerry went on to share,

"A few days later I talked about the dream with a cousin... He mentioned a poem of John Donne that turns on the point that, though east and west seem farthest removed on a map, they eventually meet on a globe. What therefore appears as opposites--east and west--in time, come together, if we follow one or the other long enough and far enough.

Later my sister, Diane, told me that the quickest way for anyone to reach the sun and the light of day is to not run west, chasing after the setting sun, but to head east, plunging into the darkness until one comes to the sunrise[1]*."*

I slammed the book shut and threw it to the corner of my room as if it had just stung me suddenly. I COULD NOT DO what he suggested. I WOULD NOT do it! To turn to the east meant to turn toward the scene of my daughter's accident. It was a decision that would force me to 'turn east' and face my darkness, to embrace the pain and emotion that promised to be there. It was all I could do to know her absence. To embrace it and all that might come with it seemed insurmountable.

I was desperately--almost frantically—trying to run from the pain of another heartbreak. I wanted to not feel the ache so deeply. I had no control of the moment, only my response to it. It was not just the loss of my child, but it was the loss of dreams and expectations for my child.

Over the next several days I walked past that book still lying in the corner. Each time I saw it, my mind would conjure up a new question.

What if I did 'face' the pain?
Can my mother's heart take any more?
What would happen if I walked into the darkness instead of trying to run from it? Would the morning come sooner or the grief become more tolerable?

Eventually I perched on the top stair step leading to my bedroom. I picked up the book, and continued where I left off in reading,

> "I discovered in that moment that I **had the power to choose** the direction my life would head, even if the only choice open to me, at least initially, was either to run from the loss or to face it as best I could. Since I knew that darkness was inevitable and unavoidable, **I decided from that point on to walk into the darkness** rather than to try to outrun it, to let my experience of loss take me on a journey wherever it would lead, and allow myself to be **transformed by my suffering** rather than to think I could somehow avoid it. I chose to turn toward the pain, however falteringly, and to yield to the loss, though I had no idea at the time what that would mean."[2]

He was right! The only way for me to truly find hope in this journey was to 'turn east'; to walk through the darkness to the sunrise after. For me that meant I had to take that walk that my daughter had taken that day she died.

I waited several more days before I dared to make that trek. I chose a day when I would be home alone. I wasn't sure I wanted to tell anyone of my plans just in case I decided not to go! I had already put off this walk several times before all the circumstances were right and I felt strong enough to at least try.

So I timidly started walking down our long lane. I thought it would be awful, but I found it filled with pleasant memories. Then I turned east and began the mile and a half to the country corner. As I walked I thought of Leisha; of things she had said or done, of songs she loved to sing or jokes she loved to tell. I remembered her last words to me and my last glimpse of her enjoying the day and the walk to meet a friend.

I stood at the corner where she darted across the intersection to meet Abby and instead met Jesus. I found myself pondering. Where was that Narnia door that had opened for her to pass through? I longed to find it, hoping that I could go too! That would be so much easier than being left here to feel the pain of her absence. There had to be a portal that we could not see, but she witnessed firsthand.

At Leisha's memorial service, a friend had shared that he could imagine her almost tripping into heaven and falling to her knees and saying, "Ooops! My bad!" I could see her doing that.

But as I now stood at this spot, I sensed that as she passed into heaven's home, she was instantly aware that she stood before the Son of God and fell to her knees in humble worship. I recalled the words of Revelation chapter 1, where John, the author of the book, writes about a vision where he finds himself at the throne of God. He sees the Lord and says,

> *17 When I saw him, I fell at his feet as though dead.*

Yes! That's how I envisioned Leisha. We saw her as if dead, but the Lord saw her very much alive, and very aware that she was in the presence of the Lord. He spoke to her.

> Then he placed his right hand on me and said: "Do not be afraid. I am the First and the Last. **18** I am the Living One; I was dead, and now look, I am alive for ever and ever! And I hold the keys of death and Hades.[3]

I remembered the description of the throne in Revelation chapter 4 as it talked about a *rainbow that shone like an* **emerald** *encircled the throne.*

Of course it would be green. Green was her favorite color. She herself had declared, "*My favorite color means my favorite word. GREEN means HOPE!*"

Chapter 4 went on to say:
> Surrounding the throne were twenty-four other thrones, and seated on them were twenty-four elders. ...In the center, around the throne, were four living creatures, and they were covered with eyes, in front and in back. ...Day and night they never stop saying:
>
> "'Holy, holy, holy is the Lord God Almighty, who was, and is, and is to come."[4]

Whatever I had believed about heaven before, in this moment at the intersection of east meets west, I sensed my daughter in the throne room, with those elders and living creatures, laying down her crown, kneeling in his presence saying, "*Holy, Holy, Holy is the Lord God Almighty, who was, and is, and is to come.*"

In this moment I knew I was also a LIVING CREATURE. I didn't have eyes in front or in back, even though there were times when my daughters were small that they were sure I must. Now I could barely see my next breath let alone my next step.

Yet I knew even in my pain, I could choose to join Leisha and give glory, honor and thanks to him who sits on the throne, to the LIVING ONE who died and now is alive forever and ever.

I fell to my knees by the side of the road where I had last seen her broken body and wept.

Over and over I repeated the words
    Holy, holy, holy,
    who was, before Leisha was born
    who is, even at this moment
    who is to come--forever and ever
    Living One who died
    Oh God!

****

I don't know how long I sat there. It seemed like hours, but was probably only a few moments. I don't remember ever noticing a car passing or a runner on the road. We may not have a lot of traffic on these country roads, but it was rare that there was no one that afternoon.

I remember standing to walk home and feeling completely spent. I didn't know how I was going to make the trek back. I had no energy for it. I began to reason, if I could make it to the next driveway, perhaps I could get the Suters to take me home.

When I got there I felt like I had enough strength to go on to the Diller's driveway. Once there, I knew that I wanted to go back over the bridge where I had last seen Leisha's vibrant smile and wave.

From there, I was sure the Basingers could take me the rest of the way. I don't remember the rest of the walk until I was walking up to the front door of my house. I collapsed on the sofa in my living room--a fragile, emotionally spent, but somehow at peace mother.

> Jerry said, "*My decision to enter the darkness had far-reaching consequences, both positive and negative. It was the first step I took toward growth, but it was also the first step I took toward pain. I had no idea then how tumultuous my grief would be. I did not know the depths of suffering to which I would descend.*"[5]

> ..."*but that is only half of the story. The decision to face the darkness, even if it led to overwhelming pain, showed me that the experience of loss itself does not have to be the defining moment of our lives. Instead the defining moment can be **our response** to the loss. It is not what happens **TO** us that matters as much as what happens **IN** us. Darkness, it is true, had invaded my soul. But then again, so did light. Both contributed to my personal transformation.*"[6]

Half the story? I trembled at what was to come. But I knew God had met me once again at that country corner. His word to me was so intimate! I had to trust he would continue to walk with me and to meet the heart cries of Rennie, Caitlin, and Brielle.

How did God show up?

I have been asked this question often by people who want desperately to know.
- How can I see God?
- Has God showed up and we missed him?
- Are we hearing from God, but don't hear because it is not what we are used to hearing?
- Could God really show up in a new way for me?

When we are in the middle of a crisis, it is so difficult to learn something new. All of our faculties are absorbed with survival. And it is almost impossible to honestly get our former knowledge about anything, but especially about God, to wrap around our emotions and our behaviors. Even though we try to do all the right things, nothing we say or do makes much sense and it doesn't make the pain go away.

For me, as the numbness of the initial shock completely wore off and the deadness of deep grief set in, I didn't feel much of anything. Nothing I did before brought me peace now.

I listened to Leisha's tapes to remember her voice or watched every video she was in. I gathered every picture ever taken of her. All of this to try to make my senses know her again; smell her, hear her, see her, touch her. In the end, there was no substitute! Nothing was adequate to fill the sense of her.

My special quiet place felt hollow, my Bible reading felt shallow, time at church felt only like programed motions. I couldn't concentrate, I couldn't process thought, I couldn't talk to God let alone hear him, nor was I altogether sure I wanted to.

My Leisha moment, or rather the journey through the grief tunnel, forced me to be born again; to learn to live all over again, to crawl, and to walk. I began with the basics like ABC's, 123's, *Jesus loves me this I know* kind of stuff.

Every day I had to learn:
- to hope
- to trust
- to live as me, only different.
- to live with all of my senses even while I feared more loss and all that came with it.

Leisha's death was a Red Sea Moment for me!

Do you remember hearing the story of the children of Israel at the parting of the Red Sea? The book of Exodus is filled with the 3 ACTS of Moses' story.

ACT 1: You can see God's hand in Moses' story all the way back to when he was born. The reigning Pharaoh declared an edict for the midwives to kill all the male Israelite baby boys. So Moses was placed in a basket and hid in the bull rushes to protect him from being discovered. **Then God showed up** with the Pharaoh's own daughter to rescue this baby and raise him as her own, allowing Moses' birth mother to be his nurse.

Later in life, Moses had to flee Egypt because he fought and killed an Egyptian slave master for whipping an Israeli slave. (Inciting Incident #1) Moses escaped to Midian, where he met and married Zipporah and had a family. **Then God showed**

up in a burning bush that didn't burn up. God gave Moses a message to go back to Egypt and free his people. (Inciting Incident #2)

ACT 2: Moses and his brother Aaron did return and gathered the people of Israel to tell them that God sent them. The children of Israel believed them. But the Pharaoh--not so much! Instead of listening to Moses, he made the Israelites work harder than ever. **Then God showed up** with 10 plagues which you will just have to read about on your own.

After a long series of requests, the Egyptian Pharaoh gave permission for the children of Israel to leave. But shortly after they left, he changed his mind and ordered his army to pursue the Israelites and bring them back--or worse, kill them.

Picture trying to move an entire community of people, only to have the whole army of Egypt with chariots and horses after you! It would be quite easy for them to catch up to...
Men
Women and children
All the livestock and animals
Carrying all the silver and gold that the Egyptians had given them
All of their clothes and baggage
And flat bread. (Want to know why? Read Exodus!)

Then God showed up! Not as he had previously in their story but in a new way. This time he came with a pillar of cloud to protect them from being seen during the day and a pillar of fire to light the way for them at night.

God told Moses what route to use. Scripture tells us he didn't lead them on the shortest route.
> *17For God said, "If they face war, **they might change their minds** and return to Egypt." 18 So **God led the***

people around by the desert *road toward the Red Sea[1].*

At one point, **God even showed up** and told Moses to turn the people back. That meant going closer to Pharaoh's army. It was not what the people wanted and seemed counter-productive for their get-away. But God had a plan. He used that move to make the Egyptians think Moses was confused. Then with assistance from the cloud he gave light to the Israelites and on the other side of the cloud brought darkness to keep Pharaoh and his army from overtaking them.

ACT 3:

Then he instructed Moses to raise his staff over the waters to divide the sea. Moses stretched out his hand over the sea, and all that night the Lord drove the sea back with a strong east wind and turned it into dry land. The waters were divided, and the Israelites went through the sea on dry ground, with a wall of water on their right and on their left. Exodus 14:21-22[2]

Imagine standing on the edge of that water bank! The waters trembled and quaked and stood to create a path through the sea, *a path no one knew was there* (Ps 77: 19). Even though they were in the middle of a miracle as the waters stood up to make a way for them, what courage it must have taken to walk with their children by their side between the walls of water wondering if the wind storm might end at any moment.

Yes, the Egyptians were pursuing them and to not cross would be death, or certainly the bondage they had just been freed from. Even with all the insecurity, going through the sea had to be the least frightening choice.

All night long the entire tribe of Israelites walk, getting all of the people through to the other side and watching as Pharaoh's horses and chariots and horsemen followed them into the path. You wonder if the children of Israel were beginning to wonder. Would you have been afraid?

But just before daybreak, as the last of the Israelites stepped out on the other side, the Lord told Moses to stretch out his staff over the sea again, and the sea went back into place. The entire army of Pharaoh was swept into the sea. Not one of them survived.

That's the Red Sea Moment.

It's a moment that is remembered over and over again, told from one generation to the next. All through scripture you see references to the Red Sea! God showed up differently than they had ever seen him before and provided something they all needed but no one could fathom. That's a story you tell your kids and they pass on to their children.

But how is Leisha's death like the Red Sea story?

Well, the most obvious reason this story struck such a chord is that Leisha's life/death is that moment for me! I tell her story again and again. I relive the memories of her death--and her life. I refer to the day she died as if it marked a beginning of a new calendar; time before Leisha and time after Leisha's death. This is my God moment I remember over and over. My Red Sea!

Another connection I make with this story is that I didn't know how I was going to get out of the grief tunnel any more than the children of Israel knew how they were going to get out of Egypt, or get through the Red Sea. **God had to show up! And he had to show up differently than he ever had before!**

He had to lead me! Sometimes it seemed like he was just being mean by not letting me take a short cut. Other times it felt like he was purposely making me take steps backward. I didn't understand. I fought his direction often, I tried to go my own way, but ultimately I came to see I had to take the path he put before me. It was a path that led through the grief tunnel. It's not a path I ever wanted to take, but it was the 'less frightening' choice.

The primary reason I felt like my story mirrored the Red Sea moment was because of the response of the Israelites after they got through it!

> *And when the Israelites saw the mighty hand of*
> *the Lord displayed against the Egyptians, the people*
> *feared the Lord and put their trust in him and in Moses his*
> *servant.*
>
> *15 Then Moses and the Israelites sang this song to*
> *the Lord:*
>
> *"I will sing to the Lord,*
>   *for he is highly exalted.*
> *Both horse and driver*
>   *he has hurled into the sea.*
> *2 "The Lord is my strength and my defense;*
>   *he has become my salvation.*
> *He is my God, and I will praise him,*
>   *my father's God, and I will exalt him.*[3]

As a worship leader myself, I have often referred back to this song as a victory celebration. Leisha's memorial service was a service of celebration led by the worship team she had just been part of the weekend before. I stood at times with my hands raised truly in worship. There were times I felt the need to take off my shoes because I was on holy ground, like Moses when he met the Lord at the burning bush.

But it struck me that while the Red Sea moment was an ACT 3 in some ways, a place of overcoming the enemy, it was also an 'inciting incident' in an ACT 1 that was to come. It spurred a journey that was yet to happen. In some ways, nothing changed within the children of Israel. After all, you can't just erase the 480 years they had been in Egypt and the bitterness that had grown with each passing generation.

They were desperately trying to leave the land, but as I read through the story again I noticed their emotions were stuck remembering what it was like to be in Egypt--pressed, pushed, driven, forced, raped of their own thoughts, feelings, emotions by the Egyptians. They went with Moses, knowing God was leading them out of Egypt, but they were still fearful, still complaining, still doubting even after the miracles they saw.

But in other ways, the Red Sea changed everything.

They had to learn to be themselves as free people.
They had to learn to trust again.
They had to learn to experience life again.

They left the oppression of Egypt only to journey through the desert. Now when they were thirsty and hungry, they had nowhere to get water or food. They doubted and complained desperately, usually to Moses. Moses would go to God.

And God showed up again. One time he turned bitter water into sweet water with a little piece of wood. He fed them with quail at night and manna in the morning--with strict instructions to rest on the seventh day, just as they had before all this happened.

Their lives had changed, their perspective on their lives and on

God had changed. But God continued to instruct them to live out their values, the principles he had taught them.

In some ways, after Leisha's death, I was the same old me! I still wore the same clothes, still lived in the same house in the middle of the same cornfield. I still had the same skills that I had before she died. I had the same stories from my past. I had the same husband and daughters (though now one was missing) and parents and sisters and brothers and friends.

But in every other way, I had to start all over.

I had to learn to breathe again, enduring the rank smell of grief. I had to learn to walk again, even as I struggled to move forward in the muck of grief.

I had to learn to see again, even as the darkness of the tunnel seemed to envelop my entire being. But I wasn't seeing with my physical eyes. No, I had to close my eyes so I could see with the eyes of my heart.

I had to learn to listen for a word, or a sound, or a song.

I had to learn to touch again; with passion for Rennie, with freedom for my girls, without overwhelming fear of losing again.

I had to learn to look for light and to feel its warmth.

When the way I used to do life failed me, or the methods I had previously practiced to seek the Lord felt empty, I began to feel like God wasn't there. I would accuse him that he had abandoned me and that I was left to find my way out of this darkness alone.

Yet just like God reminded the Israelites to remember their values from their past, gradually verses of promise I had learned even as a small child began to surface in my thinking.

Deuteronomy 31:6

*Be strong and courageous. Do not be afraid or terrified because of them, for the Lord your God goes with you; he will **never leave** you nor forsake you."[4]*

Joshua 1:5

*No one will be able to stand against you all the days of your life. **As I was with Moses, so I will be with you;** I will **never leave** you nor forsake you.[5]*

Did I believe that these were indeed promises of God? Yes! I did believe him!

Would he have lied to me when he said he would not leave me-- not ever? No! He would not lie!

He might not be there like he used to be, but I had to believe that he was showing up now. I just had to learn to NOTICE God showing up differently.

When I couldn't see him any other way, he chose to show up with GREEN. At first it was just very small traces of hope-- slivers, actually, of green hope in the dark, damp brown world of my tunnel.

For example, though Leisha chose to paint her room the hot colors of pink, orange and yellow, her favorite color had almost always been green. One day, shortly before Easter, she came home from a worship team practice at church. They talked that morning about the reasons certain colors were used to decorate the sanctuary during the Easter season.

When she got home, she came running into the kitchen and very exuberantly announced, "Mom, my favorite color means my favorite word, 'Green means HOPE!' she squealed!" HOPE! New life! Spring! Green! I loved it!

As friends and family gathered in those days after her death, story after story came out about green.

Brielle told the story of an errand she and Leisha ran together. Brie had just started driving. They had been sitting at a stop light and all of the sudden Leisha yelled, "Here it comes! It's almost here! Get ready!"

Brie frantically looked all around her, "What! What's coming! I don't see anything!"

"It's almost here! Are you ready? Are you watching? Yes! Here it is! It's GREEN!"

Yes, the traffic light had turned green!

Even though Brie had been ticked--all she could do was laugh! We've laughed about it many times since!

As we left the memorial service for Leisha, we noticed green ribbons tied to the car antennas or mirrors of everyone who had attended the service. It united us all and reminded us to live out Leisha's green hope!

So often in the last 10 years I have grabbed up everything green I can find. I have green pens and highlighters, calendars and mugs. I wear green often now, though I never used to wear green at all. I have a green Bible and a green handbag too. I even named my coaching business, *Green Hope Coaching*.

It was traces of green that first caught my attention in the darkness of the grief tunnel,

- slivers of green really as in a blade of grass

- stones of green given to me by a friend to place in a pocket or my purse. Every time I felt that stone I was reminded to notice hope.

- a broken piece of green glass that lay on the ledge of my kitchen window helping me know that though my life felt broke in a million pieces, even a small piece can bring hope and light to another.

All these greens were not just to remind me of Leisha, but rather to prompt me to notice hope; to notice when the LIVING ONE who died showed up, when God broke into my world and touched the very core of my being.

Leisha's next birthday would have been her 16th. In an effort to celebrate what was supposed to be her sweet 16th birthday and to remind ourselves to NOTICE GREEN, I declared the days between her birthday and the anniversary of her death would now be called *110 Days of Green.* Brielle even created a charcoal drawing of Leisha on green paper to commemorate the event.

So during these days from April 28th to August 16th, we looked for all the GREEN, new life, growing hope things we could find. It's not that we didn't look for those things all year round. But instead of dreading the upcoming anniversary of her death, I choose to look for the things that inspire LIFE, that empower HOPE. GREEN showed up with hope. It was a reminder that the LIVING ONE was intimately aware of the needs of my broken heart.

I told other people about it, I posted it on Facebook and wrote about it on my blog. I invited others into our 110 Days of Green with us. I begged people to share with us how Green Hope showed up in their story; to describe what hoped looked like for them, to notice where the Living One was helping them to experience new life.

I desperately wanted to know their stories. I guess in part, I was afraid I wouldn't be able to see enough hope on my own, not from the middle of the tunnel. But I know part of it was because I didn't want to be alone anymore. I needed community to come alongside and help me take my next step.

Stories began to come in. Readers shared their GREEN with me: some on the blog, others on Facebook, and some at church. It was so inspiring to have people walk up to me and say--I saw GREEN...in my child, in my front yard, in my relationship with an old friend, in my husband. Over and over we were hearing sightings of Green Hope from so many sources.

I loved it! But I knew others were benefiting from it too! Women would share how they had been encouraged when they heard another sighting of the LIVING ONE. For some it came at a crucial time when they couldn't see GREEN at all. Life was all brown, maybe even black. They needed the reminders of others to prompt them to notice as well.

I have heard from moms who have lost a child that have told me they are stuck in the death of their child--19 years ago, 35 years ago. Time has stood still for them. Their thoughts remain consumed with the death of their child. I shudder to think of the darkness of that. I know how easily I can stay stuck in Leisha's death. It's the last place I was close to her.

But I choose to remember she lived! I want to celebrate her life. I long to live out her last words to me, *"I want to influence! I want to say to people, 'I'm going! Come with me!'"* You can't invite someone to come with you if you are stuck! I could hear Leisha cheering me on!

Maybe it is not always possible to celebrate the life of a loved one because there is great pain associated with their life. I learned a long time ago there were things worse than my daughter's death. I've seen parents struggle with a child who is very much alive, but very troubled. Those are things I never had to face with Leisha.

I can't say if one loss is worse than another. Is losing a child worse than fearing for the life of a child, or the heart of a child? We really can't know that. You and I only know what we have experienced. We can only judge the level of our own pain to determine if one is more difficult for us to bear.

But no matter what kind of grief tunnel we are in, what happens to us if we become stuck in it? What happens if we allow ourselves to become accustomed to the darkness, if we stay in the trenches and continue to flail to the point we become exhausted and give up?

Where is the victory in that? What hope is in that?

What if instead we looked for hope? For me, it started with just a sliver of green. I don't know what color feels like hope to you, though when I ask people that question, they usually can tell me right away. Would God actually show up in a color? He came in a cloud and fire and a staff for the Egyptians. Why wouldn't he be able to show up in a color?

What if it is possible for hope to be green? What if it is possible for us to intentionally choose to notice hope even in the darkest days, whether it is just for today, or for 110 days or all the days for the rest of our life. The important thing is to intentionally design a way to develop your skills of noticing hope and creating ways for it to grow.

God doesn't waste anything! I long to LIVE with eyes wide open and see what it is God is doing in my world! Join me in seeing GREEN HOPE in a brown world!

16 Be Still

Our first winter after Leisha died (2006) had been almost unbearable. I'll admit, there is a lot I don't remember about that year, but I do remember Cait had jaw surgery over Christmas break and none of us felt like shopping, or baking, or decorating the house for the holidays. Those were very long, gray days trapped inside. The only way I can describe it is from a line in Chronicles of Narnia; *always winter, never Christmas.* The only good thing about that winter came in the form of a Schnoodle puppy named Lucy we got at the girls' request that Thanksgiving.

It was sometime after our first 110 Days of Green (April 28-August 16, 2007) I began to notice an intense uneasiness growing in me. Fall was here! Winter was coming!

Instead of feeling stronger as I had hoped I would by this time, I felt more fearful and more agitated by the day. I sat down one day to try to identify what was happening?   The 110 Days of Green had taught me:

- To pay attention--that had been good for me!

- To notice green--green meant hope--it was good I was looking for hope!

- To bring people into the journey with us. Yes! This is good! More people could help me find more green which meant I would have more hope, right?

- The second year of grief is sometimes harder than the first because you don't expect it to be.

Oh, the sightings of Green that people shared with me in the first *110 Days of Green* were just the thing to lift my heart. I was greatly encouraged. But if one or two green stories helped me, then what if there were 3 or 4? I began to feel as if I had to somehow generate more stories of green.

- What if I told more people about it and they were able to share more stories?

- What if I blogged about it more or asked more people on Facebook?

- What if I made my family hunt for green?

- What if I could make things green that weren't green?

- What if people forget to notice green?

- What if they forget to share?

- What if I forget to notice?

- What if I forget Leisha?

The tears flooded from a place deeper than I had ever known before! What if to not see green meant I had forgotten Leisha?

Let your heart be quiet!

My immediate response was to scream within myself, "NO! I WILL NOT LET THAT HAPPEN! I WILL NOT FORGET LEISHA."

I tried to force hope! I pasted on a smile! I felt desperate to make my family remember and do things together that they were not ready to do. I kept saying things to make other people remember, not because I wanted to be in community with them, but because I needed them to do for me what I couldn't do for myself.

Shh! My Child!

But the more I tried, the more hope seemed out of reach. I kept grasping at anything and everything that even hinted at hope. I would sit at the computer for hours looking for new pictures of Leisha hoping that by pushing her pictures a little faster I would have some relief, that some of the beauty and vitality I had seen in her that night would come back.

I watched every video of her I could find, I stalked her friends' Facebook pages hoping to find something new of Leisha to cling to. I relished every essay ever sent to me by her friends that used their perspective of Leisha's death as a topic for a class project.

Something about seeing green gave me a feeling of hope and therefore gave a bit of relief from the pain I was feeling. So I began to manipulate green in an effort to force it to show up, hoping that if I did that enough I would lessen the ache.

I was so persistent, in fact, that I went to a dollar store and picked up a silly pair of sunglasses with green lenses. They were not green frames, which would have been seen by those looking at me. I got the pair that had the green lens so I could see green while I was wearing them.

Everything I see will be green! I know--go ahead and laugh--it was a silly idea! Does it give a clue to my thought process at the time?

But I discovered something almost immediately. When I put on green glasses and tried to see through a green lens, everything -- and I mean everything--began to turn an ugly shade of puke brown. I don't know if that is an actual color, but it is not very pretty. The beautiful greens of the grass or the trees were faded by the artificial green. The blue sky turned gray, and every other color lost its richness and vibrancy. Everything became blah.

The very thing I didn't want to happen--happened. I didn't want to see any more gray days, or brown world stuff. Yet what I was reaching for was actually causing it to be true. My frantic search for green left me flailing my arms about and kicking my legs in a frenzied effort to demand that the grief tunnel release me.

Hush child!

There were times when it was all I could do to breathe, let alone move. I spent all my energy trying to do something I couldn't do. To see something I couldn't see. I would desperately try to get out of the muck, but every step only dug deeper into the darkness, and wedged me more securely into the tunnel.

It was in those moments of flailing arms and panicked breath that I had to just stop!

Stop moving!

Stop forcing yourself to breathe! Just let your body begin to function as I intended it to! Close your eyes! Let the eyes of your heart begin to see.

Finally out of sheer exhaustion, I collapsed! But as the crying quieted, I began to hear a familiar voice--not audible, but deep within me!

Be Still!

Slowly I began to notice I was still breathing. Even on the days I felt like I wanted my breath to end as Leisha's had, my body continued to take the next breath. In this moment, I was grateful

I didn't have to plan it or force it to happen. It was God-given. I was alive.

I began to see! With my physical eyes closed, sight came! It was seemingly random events here and there that left a message. Over time, each message tied together with the one before it to affirm and give credence to what God was saying to me.

I saw...Exodus 14 as the Israelites stood between the Red Sea and the Egyptians,

> [13] *Moses answered the people,* **"Do not be afraid. Stand firm and you will see** *the deliverance the Lord will bring you today. The Egyptians you see today you will never see again.* [14] **The Lord will fight for you; you need only to be still.**"[1]

Message: *I need only to be still! The Lord--the LIVING ONE WHO DIED will fight for me!*

I saw... a picture Leisha had drawn in black ink on notebook paper which was inspired by the Chronicles of Narnia! In the center was the light pole, with beams of ink streaming out to indicate the light was glowing. A dark haired girl has one arm around the pole, but faced away from the viewer as if she were looking into Narnia! Beside her were tall evergreen trees and there were footprints in the snow to show where the girl had come from.

Written within the picture were these words.

Christmas in Narnia by Leisha Burrus 12/19/2005

Hope is found, though far away in an extremely unexpected way.
Strangers fulfill a prophecy of long ago without even knowing how.

A Lion brings spring in a world frozen in time
and releases the wrath of an evil power weaker than it
knows.

Friends join together to overcome
but with the Lion, evil is completely overcome!

Hope is on the way!

MESSAGE: *Hope is on the way!   The Lion--the Living One Who Died will overcome the evil!*

I saw...Mark 1:15 *"The time has come. The Kingdom of God is near."*[2] I learned the word for time here was *kairos, not chronos* time, the sequential passing of time, one minute at a time kind of time.

But *kairos* is time outside of time when chronos stands still. It is God's time and God's watch runs much differently than ours. Kairos time is that moment when heaven touches earth and the portal between the two worlds opens to allow us to see God in a new way.

I had sensed that kind of time as I spoke to Leisha on that beautiful evening on the road, and then again minutes later when time stood still on that country corner and our friends joined us to grieve her death.

To be honest, even after all my years as a Christ follower, I struggled with this new word a great deal. Could God, who is the King of all kings and Lord of all lords, be so near, so intimately aware and involved with my personal needs and concerns? I questioned especially since the night of Leisha's accident when he hadn't shown up the way I wanted him to by giving Leisha life.

Message: *As I dared to be still, I could begin to see the many* *ways he had already broken into my world--that night and always.*

I recalled the Christmas story. Heaven touched earth the night the angels sang and a baby was born in a cattle stall to a virgin mother. I read Luke 2 again and pictured what it must have been like to live in that story. Would I have seen God breaking into my world then?

I thought back to summer camp when God broke into my world as a 7 year old. The chapel speaker had given one of those hell-fire and brimstone sermons and stated many times that there was only one way to heaven--Jesus! At the end of the evening chapel service, an invitation was given for anyone who wanted to trust Christ as their Savior. I almost ran down to the altar to be sure I had done it right enough to get into heaven.

As "every head was bowed and every eye was closed" and the last chorus of "I Have Decided to Follow Jesus" was sung, I sensed I was no longer standing at the altar by myself. I opened my eyes and looked to the floor to see shoes I knew quite well. They were my daddy's shoes.

I felt myself relax a little.

Be Still!

As the auditorium emptied, my dad invited me to sit with him on the front row of wooden chairs. He asked me why I had come forward tonight. I don't remember my specific words, but I remember how I felt saying them.

"Daddy, I'm afraid! I don't want to die and not be sure if I'm going to heaven. I don't want God to not know my name when I get there. (Yes, I know--it's a double negative. I was only 7.)

My dad put his arm around the back of my chair. *"Kathy, God doesn't want you to come to him because you are afraid. He wants you to come because He loves you. I want you to read this verse with me."*

He opened the Bible to the book of John, chapter 3, verse 16. I read these words from the King James Bible, needing a little help with some of the big words.

For God so loved the world, that he gave his only begotten son, that whosoever believeth in him, should not perish, but have everlasting life.[3]

I looked puzzled. We talked about the meaning of some of those big words like *begotten* and *whosoever* and *perish*. I knew about Jesus being God's son. I knew that he was the baby we celebrated at Christmas. I knew he was the Christ who died on the cross and who was raised again at Easter.

But then my dad reminded me that Jesus had done all of that because of love--for me! He read the verse again, but this time changed some of the words.

For God so loved KATHY, that he gave his only begotten son, that if KATHY would believe in him, she would not perish but have everlasting life.

Even as a young child, I was very aware of the difference between being afraid of God's judgement and recognizing he loved me. I was so relieved by God's love. So glad that he had loved me enough that he didn't want me to perish--so he provided Jesus!

With my dad by my side, I asked God's Son to be my Savior.

As I reflect back, I marvel that God had broken into the world of a 7-year-old girl and had spoken intimately through her father to her fearful heart. That was kairos!

Once again, I felt myself relax.

Quiet, my child!

MESSAGE: No matter the kind of moment it is, good or bad, happy or sad, long or short, when a kairos moment happens, God is close by! His kingdom is within reach as the margin between the two worlds gets thinner.

If God was that close then, that aware of me, where was God breaking into my world now? What was the kairos in this moment?

As I intentionally chose to quiet my mind, heart, body and spirit, I took a deep breath. I sensed I could quit pursuing green and just let it come to me! Every time God brought a green anything into my path, I was reminded that I didn't want to miss what God was saying. I didn't want to miss what he was trying to teach me. I didn't want this pain to be wasted. If this broken place had to hurt so badly, I wanted it to count--to purify me if that was its purpose, to teach me if I needed to learn, to be used in someone else's life if I could be used to make a difference.

Sometimes that invitation was simply to stop and be in the moment. Every time the LIVING ONE who died showed up, he brought hope with him.

Hope in the sound of Leisha's voice on her recorder or a video.

Hope in a green stone.

Hope in the notes of a friend who faithfully wrote once a week for an entire year.

Hope in a meal I wasn't expecting.

Hope in a friend who walked the lane with me.

For me, it was a miracle every time.

I felt like I had entered into death with Leisha, but I was left to be walking dead, while she was experiencing real life after her death. Yet no matter how painful her death had been and continues to be, I sensed that the intensity was just another indication of the depth of my love for her. I wouldn't give up having experienced her birth, her energy, her love for life and people, her struggle for faith and purpose, her passion for GREEN--and the hope that it represents.

I was pondering the kairos of that truth one day as I walked down our country lane and turned the corner by the mailbox to continue down the short mile we live on. It had been rare that I would take that walk since the day I had 'turned east'. It was just too hard to go there.

But this day I felt the stillness within and hope superseded despair in many ways in this fourth year of grief.

- We had painted Leisha's room--green of course, though we left hints of her original colors showing in certain places. It felt right to have her original colors peeking through.

- Caitlin traveled to Israel and Brielle to Italy for 3 months of school. They were each thriving so far from home.

- Rennie took on some new ventures with his business. It was proving to be successful.

- I started classes to get my coaching certification. By the end of my first session, I was making plans to begin my own coaching practice called Green Hope Coaching.

As I walked down the lane with our dog, Lucy, by my side, I was praying for each one of my precious family. At one point I bent down to pick a dandelion puff and tried to blow it--nothing happened. The seeds were holding tight. I thought that was odd, but held on to it as I continued to walk.

As I finished praying for Rennie, then Cait and Brie, I looked to the sky and just said, *"Lord, how I wish I could know what Leisha was doing right now. I don't know what her work is, or where she spends her time. I know you can break into my world but I wish she could. I don't even know how she looks now."*

I had often found myself watching the girls, or checking on some of Leisha's friends to see how they had changed over the last 4 years. My mom heart longed to know what Leisha would have chosen to do with her life and how she would be maturing as an adult.

"Lord, I don't know how things work now, but can you give Leisha a message from me? Could you tell her I love her and that I miss her? Tell her that I continue to pray for these people that have been impacted by her life--and her death."

Something in the clouds to the left caught my eye. As I turned to see what it was, the cloud seemed to take a shape--a human shape, more specifically the shape of a warrior standing tall and strong.

It was as if the clouds had outlined this man, including minute features of his face and hair. I was struck that his hair was almost curly, which seemed unusual for the rest of his burly appearance. He was dressed as an ancient Roman warrior with his arms at his side, and his feet in sandals with leather armor on his shins. There was a sash across his chest and something like a satchel hanging from his left hip. I stood in the middle of the road and blinked my eyes several times to be certain my eyes weren't playing tricks on me since they were cloudy with my own tears.

I looked down at Lucy. She was not paying any attention to me. I looked in front of me and behind me to see if anyone was coming on the road, but there was no one. As I looked back to the cloud, the warrior had his kind eyes focused on me.

About that time, from behind the sash on his chest, I noticed movement. Out from the satchel came a face I instantly recognized. It was Leisha! I knew her immediately. She moved very slowly at first as if she were fearful that I would not be able to handle her presence there.

I could not take my eyes off of her. She was beautiful. Her face and eyes were the same as the last day I saw her on that same road 4 years earlier, yet different. She had a confidence and a calm that only made her more beautiful. Her hair was lovely, but I could not describe it to you. It didn't seem to be important.

In a moment, Leisha raised her hand close to her face and wiggled her fingers like she used to do as if to say, "*Hi Mom!*" I sensed she was still being careful to not frighten me. I waved back in similar fashion, totally caught up in the moment.

"Leisha, is that you? Can it really be you? You look beautiful! I was just praying for you."

Leisha smiled at me, and then looked up at the warrior who seemed to nod his approval to her. She slid down from behind the sash and satchel.

"No Leisha! Don't go! Can't you stay?"

Then I saw movement again. At first I could only see her legs as if she were sitting on the cloud at the warrior's feet with one knee folded under her, and the other knee raised.

Slowly I saw her right arm lift as if she had reached behind her for something. As her hand came to land on the raised knee, her face turned into view. She smiled at me again and then motioned to the thing she was holding in her hand. It was a dandelion puff.

"Leisha! I have one too!" I raised my dandelion to show her.

She leaned into the one she held and pursed her lips together and began to blow. Seeds flew everywhere. I blinked my eyes. Is this really happening?

I instantly felt both great joy and deep sadness rush through me.

Joy because I knew what she was saying to me. Leisha was reminding me that I needed to continue to influence.

Our family had watched from the white limousine as people left the memorial service for Leisha. We saw family and friends from all over make their way out the church doors. I was struck with the thought that Leisha's influence was not just hers anymore-- or even just ours! It had been passed on to all those who had come to celebrate her life as seeds are blown from a dandelion.

Brie captured that thought in one of the paintings she did her senior year! Leisha blew the dandelion of influence, each seed turning colors as it blew away and turned into a butterfly. Each butterfly carried the name of a close friend.

Leisha was reminding me to keep influencing. I got the message at once.

But I was also filled with deep sadness because the dandelion I held in my hand had not released when I had tried to blow it a few minutes ago. In all the time I had been walking, not one seed had come off of it. My dandelion didn't work like Leisha's had.

Leisha looked at me and signaled me to blow it anyway! I did! My breath caught as all the seeds released and flew away as if they were carried by a light wind.

I don't remember when Leisha went away. I don't remember seeing the warrior or the clouds changing again or even how long it took me to get back to the house. I only know I had seen Leisha, she had spoken to me without words and I knew what to do.

I was made to influence! I needed to keep saying, *"I'm going, come with me!"*

I know! I have been skeptical in the past when someone shared a vision from a loved one. I would come up with some way their mind could have manufactured the whole thing. But I always wondered if God might actually have allowed them to experience such a personal connection.

Now God had met me in a miraculous way. This was a kairos. It was not a random moment. I have never experienced anything like this before, yet I knew that it was from the Lord. I knew that it was Leisha and I knew that her message was consistent with everything I had been hearing until now. Leisha had been real! She spoke to the core of my prayer and changed my life.

At first I was afraid to share it with Ren. What if he thinks I'm losing it? What if he tries to explain away what happened? I wondered myself if I was seeing things, if my mind was getting carried away and I was still conjuring up things just to ease the ache still present.

But as I revealed what I had seen to him, tears began to fall down his cheeks.

"Kathy, I don't know how it happened. I just know God heard your prayer and answered it in a very real way for you."

No, this is not a common occurrence. But in a precious moment, God opened up the portal from heaven and sent my daughter to me with a message tied specifically to all the other 'random' messages I had been hearing.

Be still!
Hope is on its way!
The Living One who died is breaking into my world!
Continue to influence!!

In the miracle of her birth, in the anguish of her death, and in the mystery of this moment, I have seen God bigger and more able than I ever knew him to be before.

That's a kairos!

But that is only half of the story!

Letter to Leisha on the 6th anniversary

Thursday, August 16, 2012

Hi Sweetheart!

It's been so long since I've touched you last. Six years ago today in fact! In some ways it feels like yesterday, but in most ways it seems like a lifetime ago already.

I think of you every day--wondering what life is like in heaven, knowing that your LIFE is full of richness and amazement.

- I'm wondering what kinds of things you DO there
- what WORSHIP is like when you are so aware of HIS presence,
- what WORK is like when you love what you are doing.

Even as I think of those things, I realize that even here on earth I have experienced God's presence in worship and I do know what it is like to love my work. Yet I long to know what you now know, seeing it from the other side.

This morning, Jerry Suter asked your Dad and me to come to share 'WORDS OF WISDOM' with the Suter bunch. I remember when you and your sisters would come home from picking corn and share something that was said at the WORDS OF WISDOM time. What a cool thing Jerry and

Nancy have done there--with so many kids for so long. Catherine was there, so was Jennifer and Ava and others you would know.

Dad had to leave before the kids got back from the cornfield, so I shared myself. I remembered a time when I was their age and had been asked to write my obituary. I remember being very challenged by the exercise to consider what I wanted people to say about me when I died. I wrote that I died very old, had a husband that adored me, had kids and grandkids that loved me dearly, and I did ... lots of different things that made a difference in people's lives. Nowhere did I write that I would experience pain, or lose a daughter before she had a chance to grow old.

I told them today was your 6th anniversary in heaven. I shared with them the legacy you left me. In our conversation just minutes before you died, you told me, "I want to influence. I want to say to people, 'I'm going, come with me!'" Your words became a huge impetus for me to keep moving forward so I could say to people "Come with me!" You reminded me that your favorite color means your favorite word, "Green means HOPE!" You left me a legacy of hope--green hope in a sometimes brown world!

So I challenged them to consider what legacy they are leaving in their world.

Yes, Jerry cried! You knew he would! I told the kids that the evening you died, I didn't remember all the hugs I got that night, but I remembered looking up into Jerry's face shortly after I got to the scene, and seeing in his face that he knew something about my future that I didn't know. I watched him fall to the ground in grief, sobbing not just for you or for us--but for Tim and his family all over again. I'm sure you and Tim have talked about us often. Oh, how Jerry and

Nancy have mentored us with hope--and the ability to continue to influence the lives of others for hope!

Since Dad had to leave, I didn't have a ride home! Nancy offered to take me, but I said, "I think I need to take the walk home!" She immediately knew what I was saying! "Time to think, huh?"

It was! Walking home from Suters means walking to your corner! The one where you found the Narnia door to heaven! The last time I walked there was a couple of months after you died. Jerry Sittser, in his book, "A GRACE DISGUISED" talked about early in his grief, he tried to lasso the sun and keep it from going down in the west. His sister challenged him to let go of the sun and 'turn east'. If you walk into the darkness, the morning will come sooner. At first I hated that idea! Turning east from our house meant turning toward your corner. But after thinking about it awhile, it seemed important for me to do. So one afternoon, I walked your 'last walk'; down the driveway, past Richard's barn, across 696, past Drew and Angie's, all the away to Road 5.

I didn't remember the walk back from the corner that day. My grief was so raw, the darkness so encompassing. But today I felt the warmth of the sun on my back; I was amazed at the brightness of the day and the lightness of my heart. I actually walked around the corner and suddenly stopped and looked back. I realized that my thoughts were not on the accident or your death, but your life. Times we had as a family riding bikes on that road. (Remember when Brie crashed into the ditch when she didn't know how to use her brakes yet?) So many times we drove that road to church or practice or ...to work at Suter's! I stood there and realized that as I turned the corner I was thinking of LIFE! I marveled at the healing that has come. Six years ago I never thought I would laugh again, or know joy again. I never thought I would enjoy life. But I am! You are a big part of helping me get to this place! Your legacy has reminded me to look to the ONE that can give hope!

As I walked in the door, I burst into tears and sweat poured from me! But after sleeping for a while, I realize that it wasn't the exercise that exhausted me (though I know I am not in good shape yet), it was the release of emotions that have been building over the last few weeks of preparing for the LEISHA'S HOPE event in July and looking toward this anniversary. Just because I am experiencing hope--doesn't mean I don't miss you terribly! I do! It doesn't mean I don't wish that you were still here, being part of our lives in a physical sense. Though in so many ways I sense you are continuing to make this journey with us in spirit!

This afternoon I went to the Deep Woods to meet Tabby, who was in the Jr. High youth group when you were a Sr. High team leader. Oh it was so good to see her! I showed her the FAITH cabin (she was impressed--wants to bring her folks). I showed her where the HOPE cabin will be. She loved it! We walked around the trail and talked for 2 hours. We could easily have talked more, but she had a 4:00 appointment.

One of the things I told the Lord recently was that I was sad that I don't get to see 'new' pictures of you like I do Cait and Brie. Or hear new stories of things you've said and done. But Tabby shared with me something I don't think she ever told me before. She shared with me that the evening you were on your walk, you called her and left her a message. Something like, "Hey Tabby, I just wanted to tell you that I'm not coming to youth group tonight. But I wanted you to know I was thinking about you. I'll see you Sunday!"

Tabby said she didn't know what made you think of her, but

the fact that you called her and then died has made such a difference in her life. She told me that often when she doesn't know what she should do, she thinks, "what would Leisha do?" One time after she got her new little GREEN VW Bug for graduation, she didn't want to get it dirty. Some of the kids from youth group needed a ride. Her dad just said, "What would Leisha do?" She turned to the group and said, "Ok guys, come on, let's go!" She even put the GREEN HOPE eye on some TOMS shoes that she had special ordered.

I did remind her that from your perspective now, you would remind her that it doesn't matter what you would do. What is important is what Jesus would have her do in this moment! I also reminded her that you would tell her not to be like you, but to be the very best Tabby that God created-- with all of the incredible skills and abilities and dreams that God planted in her. And Leisha, Tabby is amazing! I love her heart for her family, for people, for the 'behind the scenes' of ministry. I know God is using her in amazing ways already. He used her in my life today.

I just want you to know how very much I miss you! How much more I love you! How proud I am of you and the legacy you left for me--for so many others! Thank you honey! Have a great day in heaven today celebrating your 6th anniversary of running into His arms! I look forward to the day I will see you again!

I love you!
Mom

17 I'm So Angry

Have you ever had one of those times when the strength of your emotion was so great that it overwhelmed you and sent tears rolling down your cheeks and goosebumps up your arms? You know those times:

- when you are holding your new little one in your arms and look deep into their eyes and it's as if they can see deep into yours.
- Or when you are wrapped in your lover's arms and he looks at you with sweet tenderness and says, "I'd marry you all over again!" And you know he would--and you would too!
- Or your adult kid comes home and says 'thank you for everything' and you know they mean it with all of their heart!

Those would be some of those kairos moments we mentioned in the last chapter. But this isn't one of those chapters. The sensation I was experiencing wasn't any of those things! In fact, it was just the opposite. It was a season of kairos moments--but they were filled with intense anger.

You must know that times like these are rare for me. Oh, I get emotional--intensely emotional about a lot of things, but I'm not typically an angry person. It takes a lot for me to get angry and even more for me to discuss that anger with someone else. So the fact that I'm writing about it here means it was a big deal!

I mentioned in the last chapter that when I chose to be still
1. I realized I was still breathing--alive.
2. I began to see things--notice ways that God was showing up and the messages he was giving me.

But something else happened when I finally let go of the striving. What happens when any of us stop long enough to acknowledge how great the pain is?

3. We feel!

I was already frightened to my core by the emotions I was feeling. But to think that I was going to have to feel the complete weight of it was unbearable. I often told myself to keep moving, keep going thinking I could pretend that it doesn't hurt so bad, mostly because I could keep the emotions at a distance, desperately trying to free myself from them.

I've had lots of people tell me that I just needed to get to work in the middle of my grief. Honestly, I couldn't! Rennie went back to his work; the girls went on with school. I tried to do something, but there was little I could wrap my head around in those early days.

After Leisha died, I rarely put myself in any position where I had to be accountable to someone else for anything, not schedule or commitments or money. I had lived most of my life in public, as a preacher's kid and then a preacher's wife. I just wanted to be left alone. I didn't know if I could do grief right and I didn't want to do it wrong with other people watching. I definitely didn't want to hurt anyone else through it. I often sat with my grief alone.

Fortunately I had friends who would not leave me alone. They came to me and said, "I love you." "I'm here!" They affirmed I was not going crazy. They didn't condemn me for my grief, but continued to remind me that there is not a wrong way to grieve;

there is not a right way to grieve. We each have our own way and I needed to give myself permission to do it the way I needed to do it right now.

I remember in college reading the book *On Grief and Grieving*[1], where the authors identified the 'five stages' of grief: denial, anger, bargaining, depression and acceptance. I recognized early in my grief that these are not 'stages" because no two people ever grieve the same way. I can't 'Life Map' out my grief in some linear fashion because grief is as unique as people are. But the emotions are common to all of us as we go through loss.

Even though I most often referred to grief as a tunnel of mud, I also felt a sensation of being lost at sea; not drifting, not even in a boat, but having been shipwrecked by a storm and I was swept off into the sea, thrown about in the turbulence frantically trying to keep from drowning.

Anger became a 'structure' of some sort, as if a broken piece from the hull of the boat floated nearby. It was all I could do to grab it and throw myself on. It was something to hold on to. The anger seemed better than nothing.

At the same time, I began to feel all the other things pressing in on me:
> Darkness
> Pressure
> Fear
> Pain
> Ache
> Fatigue
> Loneliness
> Sadness
> Grief

I get that is why people don't want to *be still*. Why would we intentionally put ourselves in a place where we will feel all that pain at once? What do we do with all of those emotions when we tend to know more about suppressing them than feeling them, let alone embracing them?

The thing about this time of my life wasn't that things were going bad--in fact, things were going fairly well.

Business was good! The guys that were working with Ren had been such a help and it was amazing to see all they could do in a day!

The girls were doing quite well and often we just enjoyed being together.

I was on the worship team at church. There's not much I love more than being with a group of people who are worshiping as they lead others in worship. It is life-giving!

Ren had spoken several times at our church. It was great to see him preach again--not just hear him. I SAW him being confident of his message. I SAW him engaging more relationally with the people than ever before. I SAW his eyes filled with energy and sparkle. He loved it again! It had been a long time coming.

But as time went on, I noticed I was STOMPING. I went for a walk in the evenings, usually a pleasant experience, but I noticed now that each step was a STOMP! I was STOMPING down the lane with great agitation.

Why am I mad? Why do I feel this way? Things are going great, aren't they?

...AREN'T THEY?

At first, I blamed Rennie for my anger. I'm mad because I'm afraid he's not listening close enough to the Lord. What if God calls him to preach again and he misses it? What if we're stuck in this limbo of careers forever? Now don't get me wrong. I really am ok with Ren *fixin' on* cars for the rest of his life. I know that God is using him right now and that business can still be ministry. But I also know that part of God's design on him was opening the Word and helping people SEE it clearly. Where does God want to use that part?

Then I blamed my health coach. I have reasons to be angry. No, it's not about trust and control, well, ok, maybe a little. Well, maybe a lot--but I have reasons.

Then I made a list of ALL the other things I could think of that I was angry about--and yes, lack of world peace made the list. It was a really long list. I was appalled at all the things that made the list.

I was angry at:
- every family who had their family.
- every mom who complained about a child not showing up on time, or picking up their room.
- every dad that griped about their kid not getting good grades or putting a dent in the car!
- a mom who was angry at a kid who did something stupid and could have died. Ok there is a time to deal with it, but right now they need to know you love them and you have the privilege to still be able to tell them.
- people who insinuated how to grieve.
- people who gave trite answers to my pain, or to anything.
- people who were afraid to let me talk about Leisha.
- people who tried to pretend it was going to be ok.

I was especially angry every time someone shared one of my favorite verses. Jeremiah 29:11 (NIV) *"For I know the plans I have for you,"* declares the Lord, *"plans to prosper you and not to harm you, plans to give you hope and a future."*[2]

I had always loved this verse. I had used it to 'encourage' others! But now the last thing I wanted to hear was my daughter's death was part of "God working all things for our good!" or part of the "plans I have for you to prosper you!"

Why did my daughter have to die for good to happen? I would rather have had her living with me. She was doing well in her life. She was influencing people to see God. I couldn't see good in this moment and I didn't want to. I was too full of pain, ache, and heartbreak.

Remember earlier I said I'm not typically an angry person. Or am I?

I knew I wasn't done with the list but the relief I felt from just 'getting it out there' was so huge, I felt it physically. Being angry takes a lot of energy. But when I woke the next morning, when I started sorting out all the things I saw, one thing stood out as if it was a neon sign.

I was mad at me!

I was blaming everyone else for everything else, but what I was really mad about was that I had not listened the day Leisha died when she had asked me to take her out for coffee.

My immediate thought had been 'Why not?' But my practical side won out and I said, "We've been gone most of the day. I need to do a couple of things first. How about we leave early for youth group and I'll take you out for supper?"

So she went for a walk.

By the time we could have been sipping our favorite brew she was in the presence of the Lord.

I was mad because I heard the Spirit say, "Why not take her?" I knew inside that it was a good thing to do. But I compromised and put it off for a while. I was listening but I missed it. If I had listened and obeyed immediately, would she still be here?

Now I don't need you to send me an email with any of the platitudes we say to people when they need to remember that God is in control.Or if it was Leisha's time to die...! Or whatever! That's not what this is about!

But I knew that this was the root of my anger!

People have often asked how I dealt with my anger toward the driver of the car that hit Leisha. I've really pondered that because I have never felt anything but sadness that he and his family had to witness, or be part of, the event. I don't know why our families were connected at that country corner, but I prayed for them almost every day those first few years, and nearly every week since. I wished I could blame him at times, but I knew it was not his fault.

The layer of anger directed at Leisha didn't come for a long time. I don't know if I just couldn't bring myself to be mad at her or if that would make it too painful.
- Why did she run out in front of a car?
- Why didn't she pay attention?
- Why couldn't she be content at home?
- Why did she go for a walk that day?
- Why didn't she wait for me to take her?

That led me to question if my action precipitated the accident. Did I cause this? When our family was dealing with the repercussions of our perfect little lives, I had to come to grips with my role in our situation. Some of it was my fault then, how much of it was my fault when Leisha died? I became consumed not only with my feelings about Leisha, but about past mistakes and sinful behaviors. The weight of guilt and shame took me to my knees.

The thing about the anger is that while I have *put it into a chapter,* it did not happen so neatly. The anger was tangled with so many other emotions like shame, guilt and fear. Yet the anger forced its way around situations and relationships and would snap at me when I least expected it.

Often when those emotions are stirred I try to analyze why they happened so I can ensure that they will never happen again. For a while I deflected my anger at myself to God. Why didn't YOU do something? You knew this was going to happen? You could have stopped it! Why didn't you?

All the while knowing at some point I had to deal with my anger with myself!

It was on a coffee date with my friend Barb that I finally confessed the shame, guilt and anger I felt for having let my girls down. It wasn't just disappointing them, it was life altering stuff. I talked about all the situations I had failed to do the right thing and all the relationship issues I could have avoided if I had obeyed the promptings of my heart. I was exhausted when I finished the list of grievances against myself as I sat back in the booth.

Barb let the moment settle a bit, and then she leaned into the table, and asked, *"What would happen if you embraced that shame, the guilt, the anger and brought it in close?"*

I could barely breathe at the thought of it, tears filled my eyes. *"I can't! It hurts so bad the way it is."*

She softly whispered, *"What if instead of trying to shoo it away, which means you have to address the emotions over and over again, you reached out and grabbed them and drew them in to let them do their worst to you? What is the worst that could happen?"*

I wasn't sure, but the risk seemed too great! She assured me that was ok! When I was ready and able, I would know what I had to do.

I thought back to the verse in the Mark 1 passage we talked about in the last chapter. *"The **time** has come'* Jesus said. *"The Kingdom of God is near."*[3] This was one of those times! God was near; he was doing something in me. But it dawned on me that the verse doesn't end there. The next part reads, *"Repent and believe the good news!"*

Was that what 'embracing' these emotions meant?

When we repent, we *"feel sorry for, or regret"*. (dictionary.com) But just feeling sorry for something rarely is impacting enough to create lasting change in us. In Mark 1, the original meaning of repent more closely resembles the Amplified Bible's definition.

Change your inner self—your old way of thinking, regret past sins, live your life in a way that proves repentance; seek God's purpose for your life. (biblegateway.com)[4]

So, to repent I needed to own my past and my old way of thinking and make a change which results in new ways of behaving. That had to begin with embracing the emotions I feared most.

Admitting my anger, much less all the other emotions, was very difficult to me. I came to own that I had been angry for a long time, probably even before I got sick or we entered into family counseling. But I felt like I *should not* express that anger because too many people were already angry. Someone had to have grace! So it would be me!

I also realized I was really good at REPENTING, recognizing that God was calling me to do something differently. I repented, got honest with myself about my anger, figured out why it made me feel a certain way. I even shared my reflections with a trusted friend who was willing to let me be real.

But too often I quit there--admitting I was angry. I felt regret for my thoughts and often my behavior. I learned that something needed to change. Isn't that enough?

I would hurry off to the next thing, without following through on making any change on the first thing. I often wondered why it felt like I was being forced to learn lessons over and over and still not seeing any fruit.

Then I was reminded that becoming aware of the issue is only half of the learning God has for us. REPENT *AND* BELIEVE. That's the second half of the 'good news'.

Dictionary.com tells us that to BELIEVE *is to have confidence in the truth, the existence, or the reliability of something.*

Truths I learned as I repented were given to me to act on. That action shows that I believe it. What was the action I sensed God was asking of me?

Remember the story of Charles Blondin, the tightrope walker who became the first person to cross a tightrope stretched across the Niagara Falls? People came from all over to watch him cross over these waters on a quarter of a mile of rope on stilts or a bicycle, in the dark and even blindfolded. Once he carried his manager across riding piggyback. I've heard the story told with other things he might have done, but suffice it to say, he did accomplish some very bold adventures.

The story goes on to say that the crowd ooo'd and aah'd each time with growing amazement. Then he asked the audience, "Do you believe I can carry a person across in this wheelbarrow?"

The crowd enthusiastically yelled, "Yes! You are the greatest tightrope walker in the world. We believe!"

"Okay," said Blondin, "Who wants to get into the wheelbarrow."

As far as the Blondin story goes, no one did at the time![5]

That was me! I believed I had learned something, and that God was speaking to me about my intense emotions. But I wasn't willing to act on it. Right now it seemed I needed to grab hold of my anger and let it do its work in me.

As Barb and I parted ways that day outside the coffee shop, I cried my way to my car. She was right. I had to deal with this. Every time I threw up my hand to shoo it away, my fingertips touched the emotions all over again. I kept opening up the wounds and they would never heal this way.

I looked at myself in the rear view mirror. *Kathy, what is the worst that could happen? The pain you feel is so great now, it has to get better and not worse.* I reached out my hand. I closed my fingers around all the shame, guilt and anger. I pulled it close to my heart and wept at the pain I felt responsible for. I whispered the words, "God! I'm so sorry! I believe you! Please forgive me!"

In an instant I knew he already had!

I opened my hands and felt the release of my faults to the Living One Who Died for those sins. He had already paid the price for them. I just hadn't released these to him. I drove away amazed at the difference of my heart and eternally grateful for the forgiveness of a God who loves me--and my daughters more than I do.

Do you remember a time when you've been really sick, not necessarily just a few hours, but for days--or maybe you were going through a very difficult time? Maybe there was a relationship that was struggling or a circumstance that was eating your lunch.

Remember how hard it was to get through those days? How it seemed to take all the effort you could muster just to get your feet on the floor in the mornings. It felt like you carried 1000 tons of heaviness.

That's not the feeling I want you to remember.

I want you to remember the feeling you had that morning when you woke up before the alarm, you rolled over, and sat on the edge of the bed. It dawned on you that you felt better. The achiness was gone and the brain fog seemed to have lifted. You felt ready for a new day.

Or perhaps a relationship issue was resolved or the circumstance changed somehow for the better. And you noticed that you almost slid out of bed and you made your way to the kitchen for that first cup of coffee and 'oh, it tasted extra good.' You stepped outside and breathed in deeply.

Do you remember what it felt like to have the fresh air against your skin and the warmth of the sun on your face?

229

THAT'S THE FEELING I WANT YOU TO REMEMBER!

That moment happened for me one Sunday in June 2011 as I led worship. It was the first weekend of our *Summer Breeze* series.

That summer at church we were using the BREEZE to represent the Spirit of God that was at work in and around us. The beauty of being on the worship team is that I have two rehearsals and three services to sing these songs. Often as I become comfortable with how to sing the song then I am free to pay attention to what I'm singing. My worship comes from a very real, very fresh place in those moments.

This particular weekend, we sang a song our Worship Pastor Jason had written called WIND OF GOD.

> *Wind of the Spirit, blow through my soul*
> *Come and renew me; come make me whole*
> *Fire from heaven, purify my heart*
> *Come and refine me, take me to where You are[1]*

As we sang the chorus for the second time that morning, I began to notice a fresh breeze blowing against my face. It was so evident that it caught me by surprise and for a moment I had to stop singing. It was not a gust of wind as if someone opened a door and wind blew in. This was a gentle breeze that could be explained no other way than God showing up. It was different than the air I had been breathing in the grief tunnel for so long. It was renewing! I could breathe it in. It was fresh and cool--more real than ever before.

I couldn't imagine ever feeling that way again. I had been in the grief tunnel for five years where it was dark and musty; sometimes I felt like I was under the mud and couldn't breathe at all.

But here I was--breathing fresh air, breathing life!

As I stood with my face lifted and my arms flung back drinking in the breeze, the phrase that kept coming to my mind was, *I AM the resurrection and the life.*[2]

That powerful truth in that single phrase kept replaying in my mind as I left the church and all through lunch with Rennie. That afternoon, I grabbed up my Bible and took another look at that passage found in John 11. The words seemed fresh, as if I were reading them for the first time.

I was struck how John's version of this story connected with my experience during the last five years. I was most taken by each character's reactions to Jesus in this moment. Suddenly this was not just a Bible story. These were real stories of ordinary people just like me.

Over the next few days, I pondered each character closely. First there is Lazarus who lives in Bethany and is a follower of Jesus. In this story he is so sick that his sisters sent a message to Jesus and said, "The one whom you love is sick". Another translation says "Your dear friend." So Lazarus was not just a fan, but a friend!

He is also a brother to Mary and Martha. Remember them? In Luke 10 Jesus stopped by their home for a meal. Martha had gotten pretty miffed at Mary because instead of helping Martha in the kitchen, Mary sat down at Jesus' feet and listened to His teachings. That left Martha to fix the meal and oversee the preparations all by herself.

Martha tells Jesus to tell Mary to come help in the kitchen. I'm guessing Martha knew if Jesus set Mary straight, then Mary would get the scolding she deserved. I wonder if big sister might have hoped Mary would feel a little embarrassed about not helping as she should have.

But Jesus doesn't tell Mary to help. In fact, he says, *"My dear Martha, you are worried and upset over all these details! ⁴² There is only one thing worth being concerned about. Mary has discovered it, and it will not be taken away from her."³*

But...the Luke 10 story is not the story I'm here to tell.

In John 11, Jesus is already on his way see Lazarus, Mary and Martha again when the sisters send him a message telling him that Lazarus is very sick. You would think Jesus would have made every effort to get to their home quickly. But John writes, *"So although Jesus loved Martha, Mary, and Lazarus, he stayed where he was for the next two days."⁴* Then Jesus says something to the disciples about the illness not leading to death and God would be glorified through it.

You know, I really struggled when people said that to me after Leisha died. I knew then and know now that God was and is at work through all of the Leisha story. But why should I feel good that God would be more glorified through her death! Leisha was growing in her relationship with the Lord. Her life was glorifying God too. I would have rather had her with me all these years.

Yes, that probably sounds pretty 'unspiritual'! But when I was in the deepest part of my grief, the fact that God would get glory was secondary to the level of pain I was feeling because of her absence. I wondered if the disciples were confused by Jesus' words and behavior too.

Finally Jesus says, *"Let's go to Bethany!"* But by the time he gets to their home, Lazarus has already been dead four days. This is where it gets interesting to me. Look who is the first person who comes to meet him.

MARTHA

[20] *When Martha got word that Jesus was coming, she went to meet him. But Mary stayed in the house.* (Notice Mary doesn't go!) [21] *Martha said to Jesus, "Lord, **if only you had been here**, my brother would not have* died."[5]

If only! Oh! I've said those words so often.
> If only Leisha were still here.
> If only God would have kept Leisha from running out in front of the car.
> If only I had not talked to her at all that day or talked to her longer.

I wondered if Martha was really saying,
> If only you would have been here.
> If only you could have done your miracles like you have for so many others.
> If only you would have been for us who you said you are!

That's what we do when our hearts are broken and life is painful. We begin to criticize, even accuse, the very one who could do something about it.

She does go on to say, *"But even now I know that God will give you whatever you ask."*
When Jesus tells her, *"Your brother will rise again!"*
Martha says, *"Yes, he will rise again when everyone else rises, at the last day!"*[6]

Don't you wonder if that Luke 10 scene is replaying in her mind about now? She was working so hard to serve that meal to Jesus as her guest that day. She gets a bum rap so often because she 'chose the wrong thing', but I believe she wholeheartedly wanted to honor Jesus. It was just that somewhere in the doing, her focus became more about getting the tasks done and less about doing it because she was in relationship with Jesus. At that visit Jesus told her that she missed the most important thing.

In this moment, she had to be wondering, "Am I missing it again? I KNOW that he will rise again. I KNOW that, right?"

That's when Jesus told her, "[25] ***I am the resurrection and the life.** Anyone who believes in me will live, even after dying. [26] Everyone who lives in me and believes in me will never ever die. Do you believe this, Martha?*"[7]

Martha, do you believe that I am? Do you know WHO I AM?
I AM the resurrection and the life!

Martha says, *"Yes, Lord, I believe that you are the Christ, the son of the Living God."*[8]

Her answer seems confident, but I see question marks circling in her head! What is he saying? What am I missing? As I pondered Martha's response, I noticed two things:

- Martha did believe that Jesus **could have** kept Lazarus from dying, **if only** he had been there.

- She also believed that Jesus **will** raise Lazarus at the last day along with all the others he will raise--someday!

Those are important things to believe. Martha knew there would be a resurrection. She believed that! She just couldn't bring herself to hope that Jesus could do anything now that Lazarus was dead!

I pondered how LIMITED Martha's view was of Jesus who stood before her! I pictured myself standing with her. Would I have known Jesus to be the resurrection and the life? I had prayed on that country corner on August 16th, 2006, that God would raise

Leisha up at the scene of the accident. I believed he could, but he didn't. I couldn't begin to imagine how he would ever help me feel life again!

Then it occurred to me that neither Martha nor I had ever NEEDED to see Jesus BIG ENOUGH for dealing with the death of a loved one. Now we desperately needed to know him as the **resurrection and life**.

I reflected on the fresh breeze I had felt during worship moments earlier that week. Over the past five years I had seen him bigger than I had ever known him to be. He had shown up to be MORE than I could have ever imagined him to be. When he did he brought hope with him. So much hope that I was experiencing life again.

Martha and I were both seeing Jesus bigger than we had ever known him. I wondered, *'Do I know Jesus to be who he says he is? Do I believe Jesus is the resurrection and the life in other areas of my life?'*

And then there is MARY

Mary pulls at my heart in a different way. She had chosen to sit at his feet the last time he visited, but did you notice Mary didn't go out to meet Jesus with Martha?

Maybe she didn't have the strength to deal with all the drama of her 'older bossier sister.' Maybe!

Maybe Mary was just numb with grief? I so get that! Sometimes when we are in so much pain, we cannot do the thing that might be considered good etiquette.

But could it be that she was angry at Jesus? She had this special relationship with him so why didn't he make more effort? Why didn't he choose to come to them sooner?

I don't know why Mary doesn't go to see him right away, but when she does see Jesus, scripture says *she fell at his feet and said, "Lord, **if only** you had been here, my brother would not have died."* [9]

There they are again, those two little words. **If Only!** Mary said virtually the same words as her sister! I once read, '*they said the same thing--don't read too much into this."* Really?

Ok, I'll admit the sisters have had four days of conversation since Lazarus died. Sometimes we might say something the same after we have talked about it with others for a while.

But Martha is the oldest. She has the responsibility of hospitality and food preparation, (we see that in the story of the visit Jesus had with them earlier) as well as, overseeing the gathering on this sad day. Greeting Jesus would be one of her responsibilities. She's quite driven by details for the sake of a task. Also, John doesn't make a point to tell us that Martha fell at Jesus' feet. Most likely she stood to talk to him.

And Mary? Well, this is the same Mary that Jesus says 'chose the better thing!' (Luke 10:39). Her personality is passionate and she values the *relationship* she has with Jesus enough to once again fall before him when she sees him. Even if she was upset with him, she still responded out of her natural design.

These sisters may have said the same words, but they *ain't sayin'* the same thing! They have dealt with everything else differently. I have to believe these words are going to mean something different now as well.

I hear Mary saying, with great disappointment in her voice, "Lord, You messed up! You failed me. I chose you, why didn't you show up when I needed you?"

I can imagine that when she sent for Jesus, her relationship with him caused her to believe he would be there for them in this situation. But she also seems to have expectations of HOW Jesus would respond, HOW he would answer her 'prayer' and demonstrate his deep love for her family by keeping Lazarus from dying.

I choked on that thought. That was me! I had worked hard to honor the Lord my whole life. Perfectly, no! But I had been a student of the Word and a worshiper of the Lord. I worked hard to develop a relationship with him that was close and personal.

Yet there's a sense in which the deeper the intimacy we have with God, the more vulnerable we are to disappointment with him. His *perfect* love doesn't always take the form we assume it will. Or at least what we think it should! I didn't think I was serving him for what I could get, but it was beginning to appear that I had selfish motives.

In a phone call with my friend and mentor, Becky Harling, she reminded me: *"God never promised to spare me, or to spare you from suffering. He only promises to be with us **in** our suffering."*[10] *(Finding Calm in Life's Chaos, pg 98)*

When I was letting go of my perfect little life, I thought I had let go of the mindset that if I did enough right things God would bless me. To me that meant he would make our ministry flourish and protect my kids, and keep us healthy. God never promised that!

But God did say: Isaiah 43

> *"Do not be afraid, for I have ransomed you.*
>
> *I have called you by name; you are mine.*
>
> **² When you go through deep waters,**

I will be with you.
When you go through rivers of difficulty,
you will not drown.
When you walk through the fire of oppression,
you will not be burned up;
the flames will not consume you.
³ For I am the Lord, your God, the Holy One of Israel,
your Savior...because you are precious to me.
*You are honored, and **I love you.***
*⁵ "Do not be afraid, for **I am with you.**¹¹*

I considered how I, like Mary, had expectations of how God was going to work in my life and in my tragedy. I asked myself, *Do I DARE to trust him if he shows up in ways I don't EXPECT?*

Then I see JESUS

³³ When Jesus saw her (Mary) weeping and saw the other people wailing with her, a deep anger welled up within him and he was deeply troubled. ³⁴ "Where have you put him?" he asked them.

They told him, "Lord, come and see." ³⁵ Then Jesus wept. ³⁶ The people who were standing nearby said, "See how much he loved him!" ³⁷ But some said, "This man healed a blind man. Couldn't he have kept Lazarus from dying?"¹²

At first I wondered if it was because Jesus was angry at himself. He could have gotten there sooner to keep Lazarus from dying. But several times scripture indicated that he knew all along what was going on. But it says he was *Deeply troubled*? Deep anger wells up within him? I don't often think of Jesus that way.

Then I thought what it was like to be him in this moment! He was surrounded by these friends, followers, people who said they knew him. They declared that they **BELIEVE** that Jesus is *the Christ, the Son of the Living God.* Martha said it too! Yet here they are looking at him with uncertainty, overcome with grief.

All of the time he spent in relationship with them, yet they didn't see him for who he really was! ***The One*** *in whom victory, life and resurrection are all powerful realities.*[13] All this time he's been trying to tell them who he is, but in their pain either they can't see it, or it seems too hard to believe. Jesus didn't come as they expected him to.

And then his anger turned to tears. Seeing their grief, he grieved with them. Two little words suddenly became two of the most powerful words to my own grief.

Jesus wept.[14]

He didn't just shed a few tears! He wept crying out of the soul, sobbing. Jesus! With an ugly cry! I began to fathom Jesus is angry at death, He is angry at how devastating death is in the lives of these people he loves.

It was in that moment that I let down more barriers in my heart--walls that had been protecting me from a God who allowed Leisha's death to be part of my story. I saw Jesus see me! Feel with me! Cry with me! Walk with me through the cornfield at that country corner the night of the accident.

I visualized myself crawling up into his lap, my tears gushing with my own ugly cry. Jesus had shown me it was ok to cry, to let my pain release through tears.

So many times we feel the need to cry ugly tears:
- Maybe it is a **loved one** who has been taken!
- Or a **relationship that is coming unraveled**--a friendship, a marriage, a family.
- Perhaps a **safe place** has been violated and it's no longer safe and secure.
- Or your **identity** is shaken--job is taken away, confidence is gone, you mourn loss of who you were.
- Maybe it's because you're **not young** anymore. You look in the mirror and wonder how you got to be this old, not able to do what you used to do, you feel pains you didn't use to feel.

Becky also wrote in her book *Finding Calm in Life's Chaos*, *"Our Savior sees, hears, and feels our sorrow and weeps with us. He doesn't stand back aloof or arrogantly instruct us to 'stop crying' or 'toughen up!' Instead tears stream down his face on our behalf. And as we truly grieve our losses, we take a step toward healing...toward restored hope! He not only longs to bring hope back to my life--to yours...He can!"*[15] (pg. 99-100)

As my tears subsided that afternoon, I was so grateful that Jesus affirmed I not only need to grieve my losses, but it's ok to do it with an ugly cry.

I could have stopped there in my reading of that passage and had great truths to cling to in my own journey out of the grief tunnel.
- Martha: Do I know Jesus to be who he says he is?
- Mary: Do I dare to trust Jesus when he shows up different than I expect?
- Jesus: Will I allow myself to grieve, even with an ugly cry?

But it's what comes next that really stands out!

³⁸ Jesus was **still angry** as he arrived at the tomb, a cave with a stone rolled across its entrance. *³⁹ "Roll the stone aside," Jesus told them.*

But Martha, the dead man's sister, protested, "Lord, he has been dead for four days. The smell will be terrible."

⁴⁰ *Jesus responded,* (you wonder if it should have said YELLED EXASPERATEDLY!) ***"Didn't I tell you that you would see God's glory if you believe?"***

The ultimate "I told you so!"

So they rolled the stone aside. Then Jesus looked up to heaven and said, "Father, thank you for hearing me. ⁴² You always hear me, but I said it out loud for the sake of all these people standing here, so that they will believe you sent me." ¹⁶

Jesus, the Resurrection and the Life, the Great I AM speaks directly to death. Jesus shouts with a loud voice full of authority--not just for the dead man--not just for death, but also for the crowd, the people who were standing close by.

43 "LAZARUS, COME OUT!"

Everyone there *"gasps at the audacity of Jesus' command."*¹⁷Wouldn't you?

What does LAZARUS do?

Verse 44 says **The dead man walked.**

Picture it!

Mary and Martha are standing with some close friends weeping, others are scattered nearby. Jesus walks among them and as he sees them weeping, he begins to weep. His shoulders begin to shake as the sobs grow stronger. His hands cover his face as he bends low in grief. You sense the pain that he is feeling--even though you don't understand its depth.

You can hear him cry out, "Roll away the stone!" Then you hear Martha's protest, but several me strain against its weight as they obey the command.

You see Jesus lift his face toward heaven in prayer. And then, in a powerful voice, a voice filled with authority, you hear him shout!

One that I love, come forth!

And then you hear it again! Come Forth! You try to move so you can get a better view--then realize you can't--your arms and legs are bound tightly. You lift your eyes slowly and your gaze meets his! He extends his arm toward you! "One whom I love--Come forth!"

He's talking to you. You are the one that is dead. You don't remember dying! Well, you remember feeling like dying after that tragedy that seemed to swallow you up. But you thought you were alive. You were working so hard to be alive.

Slowly you visualize parts of you that are dead. One by one, memories begin to flood your mind of deep hurts, profound loss causing wounds that would not heal relationships, emotions, and circumstances. Larry Crabb described them as *agonizing problems that generate in our souls an experience that feels like death.*[18] *(Finding Calm in Life's Chaos, 98)*

My mind paused on the thought that it was not just Leisha who died that August day. Parts of me died that day too! My heart felt like it no longer wanted to beat, yet it did. I felt like I could no longer breathe, but I did. My joy was broken, hope felt faint.

Suddenly I could SEE
- This One who is more than I have ever KNOWN
- This One who works differently than I could EXPECT
- This One who IS the resurrection and the LIFE.

He has the power over death; not just in this story but in a few weeks later at his own crucifixion if you keep reading in the book of John. This is the ONE WHO WINS! He is the LIVING ONE WHO DIED AND LIVES FOREVER (Rev 1: 17) He brings the dead to life! He has power over the grave!

That same Jesus was looking at me! "Unwrap her, let her go!"I lifted my face toward heaven and once again felt the breeze against my face.

The Living One who Died LIVES AGAIN so that I could live again with LIFE and HOPE RESURRECTED!

19 White Knuckle Fear

It would seem that once I made it out of the grief tunnel, life would be finally getting back to 'normal' (whatever normal was before you entered grief). I wish I could say that after breathing fresh air and experiencing Jesus as the resurrection and the life, that I was finished with ACT 2 and ready to start writing ACT 3-- the ending of the story.

But that is not what happened for me. At least I don't recognize it to be Act 3 yet.

Each year as the distance grew from the day of Leisha's accident, I felt like another part of me was "waking up". That should be a good thing, yet standing out in the open, free of the tunnel, actually left me feeling extremely vulnerable. As bizarre as it sounds, the grief tunnel had become a place of comfort even though it was full of pain and misery.

As I began the process of un-numbing (if that's a word) it became very apparent that I was filled with fear. In fact, I had lived much of my life AFRAID! I didn't think of myself as afraid, though there were times when I quite easily bordered on, if not plummeted into, panic. But I kept telling myself that I should cut myself some slack. There had been a lot of hard things in my life. I needed to give myself time to get over it.

But life was full of change--hard change, good change, great change even, but change none the less. Fear of CHANGE is one of the top five fears that people have. The others include: fear of failure, fear of unworthiness, fear of loss of identity, and fear of success. Death and loneliness are actually farther down the list.

Throughout my story, I have already admitted to times when all these fears have played a large role in my life. But I'm a person that works hard to process my emotions. (I'm a LIFE COACH for pity sake!) Yet I was blown away by how so many of these emotions were still playing over and over in my mind and heart even though I had already identified some of these as lies. I thought I had replaced the lies with truths that I could believe and own.

Henry Nouwen told a story of an elderly woman that was being admitted into a psychiatric hospital. *She was wild, swinging at everything in sight. The staff was so concerned by her behavior that they had to take everything away from her. But she made a fist so tight and would not give up. It took two people to **pry open her clenched hand**. In it was one small coin. It was her last possession. Her fear made her believe if they took it, she would have nothing more, she would be nothing more.*[1]

Those words penetrated a place deep in my heart.

Without knowing or intending to be, my fear had transformed me into that woman who was *wild, swinging at everything in sight*. My experience with people in the middle of grief taught me it wasn't unusual to be angry or fearful. In fact it was expected after the numbness of the loss began to wear off.

But the *ME* that I once knew was no more. I wasn't sure who I was becoming.

I was so AFRAID
- anger would win.
- I would hurt someone I love more deeply than they had already been hurt.
- I would become bitter and not be able to overcome it.
- God, who I knew to be the *Blessed Controller of all things* yet also allowed Leisha's death, might allow something more to happen.
- I would not be able to survive with this gaping hole in my heart.

I didn't want to be that woman with clenched fists flailing wildly at anyone and anything that might threaten to hurt her. Did I understand why she behaved as she did? You bet I did! But I wanted to be the woman who could *be still and know God.*

Our mind does strange things to us when we allow ourselves to be still enough to feel our fear. Our hearts begin to tense up and build walls to protect ourselves.

Our hands begin to gather those we love close to us and grab at things that seem important, things we think we can control.

We begin to squeeze so hard that our fingernails start cutting into the palm of our hands and our KNUCKLES BECOME WHITE!!!

Maybe WHITE KNUCKLE fears are linked to a specific memory. But maybe it hasn't even happened and we find ourselves fearing what could happen. When we are afraid, we let ourselves imagine some of the most horrific events.

Some of the white knuckle fears I feared most were:
Fear of losing my child
Fear of losing my husband and having to raise our children myself

Fear of messing up and screwing up my kids
Fear of making right decisions for health or discipline
Fear of current events
Fear of losing my own identity--things I love to doing
Fear of losing a relationship with lover or friend
Fear of going to work or fear of staying home
Fear of judgment of others
Fear I won't perform
Fear of our children's fears
Fear of being trapped
Fear of being abused
Fear of being betrayed

Those were the times I leaned toward becoming **that woman.** I took the stance of a fighter with fists closed and feet spread to give me some balance. But my jabs and swings were not controlled like a trained fighter. They were wild and aimed at the most recent thing that threatened to hurt me. These WHITE KNUCKLE fears kept me clenching my hands and holding on to anything I felt I could still control.

I thought about how many times I had heard the words "do not be afraid" as a child.

"Don't be afraid, honey, we will leave on a light."

"I looked under the bed already, there is nothing there. You don't have to be afraid."

I felt less afraid because my mom or dad was near or one of my four siblings was close.

But my fears only became more intense as I grew up and had a family of my own. The fact that Ren or the girls were close made me more aware of my fear, because I suddenly wasn't just afraid for me. I feared for them as well. It occurred to me that our fears often tell us what is most important to us.

Though I suppose they all play into it, the greatest fear I struggled with isn't on the list above. My greatest fear is that I will once again experience a loss
>like losing Leisha--
>or leaving ministry
>or having to let go of a dream like being a "pastor's wife".

About the time I was addressing these, my fear increased as our friend, Sarah G, passed away after a horrid struggle with cancer. She was a young mom with four little boys at home. She had also been the youth pastor's wife that meant so much to our family.

Sarah was a cherished mentor for our girls. I have written about her earlier in the book because of Sarah's importance to Leisha. They both lived passionately. They both loved people. And they both did it all with courage.

I grieved. I felt gut sick. I thought it was for her and her boys and dear husband. But my friend Pat noticed I couldn't speak of Sarah's mom, Mary. As soon as Pat mentioned her, I broke out into tears. My grief for Sarah's mom was actually the deeper grief.

Then weeks later a young woman named Jordan was killed in a single car accident. When I heard, I felt the floor rising up and my body feeling like it was collapsing. Though I stood, I was gut sick again, numb, needing to cry.

Jordan was 2 days older than Leisha. She had a painful journey in her teens, mainly through choices she made, but she had recently made some very right choices and was honoring the Lord in her life. I could think only of this girl's mother, Mandy, then of Jordan's 3 year old child.

My heart screamed, "Lord, what would happen if I had to experience loss again? Especially the kind of loss that explodes my heart with violence so great that I can't even find all the pieces let alone put them back together again? Would I be able to survive another loss like that? Can't you do something about this?"

My mind flashed back to the moment I heard a story of a man who said something similar. Linda Dillow was speaking to a group of ministry wives in Dallas, Texas. I knew enough of her story to know that there had been a time of great struggle for her several years before the Dallas event. I had been praying for her. Now, she told her story in her book, *Calm My Anxious Heart*, and introduced me to this man called Habakkuk.[2]

The story in the book of Habakkuk is all of three chapters long. The prophet Habakkuk (I'll call him HB for short) was crying out to the Lord but feeling like God was not listening. The violence and evil deeds HB witnessed every day against the children of Israel were unjust and unfair. It's a 'God, can't you do something about this' moment!

The Lord replies to him, "Look around and be amazed! I'm doing something in your own day, something you wouldn't believe even if someone told you about it."

But then the Lord begins to reveal a plan of raising up an even more cruel and violent people to conquer the land and the Israelites with it.

HB basically says, "Surely not! You can't be serious about wiping us out! Are you really going to let this happen?" He braces himself for the worst, wondering what God will say to his questions. The story says HB climbs the watch tower and waits for God's answer.

God does answer, "Yes! This is coming!" Then he describes the judgment that is to come on the captors, not on the faithful. Who do they think they are making other gods out of money, wood and stone? Yes, the children of Israel will be caught up, but only to do a greater work.

Hmm? I've never liked those kind of plots.

I don't think Habakkuk did either. But the prophet prays:

> *I have heard all about you, Lord.*
> *I am filled with awe by your amazing works.*
> *In this time of our deep need,*
> *help us again as you did in years gone by.*
> *And in your anger,*
> *remember your mercy.[3]*

HB begins to recall those stories of long ago of God's salvation for the Israelite people. He includes the Red Sea moment where God showed up bigger than they had ever seen him before and different than they expected. But He showed up! And the work He did was far greater than they could ever imagine.

HB continues:

> *I trembled inside when I heard this;*
> *my lips quivered with fear.*
>
> *My legs gave way beneath me, and I shook in terror.*
> *I will wait quietly for the coming day*
> *when disaster will strike the people who invade us.[3]*

Those words spoke of fear so similar to the fears I mentioned earlier. HB knew the kind of fear I felt. But I love what he prays next.

> *¹⁷ Even though the fig trees have no blossoms,*
> *   and there are no grapes on the vines;*
> *even though the olive crop fails,*
> *   and the fields lie empty and barren;*
> *even though the flocks die in the fields,*
> *   and the cattle barns are empty,*
>
> *¹⁸ yet I will rejoice in the Lord!*
> *   I will be joyful in the God of my salvation!*
> *¹⁹ The Sovereign Lord is my strength!*
> *   He makes me as surefooted as a deer,*
> *   able to tread upon the heights.⁴*

I was reminded of a prayer I made in a blog post three days before Leisha died.

> *What am I feeling?*
> *Is it discontent?*
> *Where do we fit?*
> *What are we to do?*
> *What's next?*
> **Can't you do something?**
>
> *Lord, you've led me to Revelation!*
> *In it I read You are the Alpha and Omega*
> *The Beginning and the End*
> *The First and the Last*
> *You are the one who is*
> *Who always was*
> *Who is still to come*
> *The Almighty One*
> *The Living One who Died!*
> **Continue to teach me about you, Lord!**

My heart lurched!

Had all the pain I experienced with Leisha's death been an

answer to that prayer? I wrestled with God from *Turning East* through anger all the way to white knuckle fear. Yes! I felt as Habakkuk

> *I trembled inside ...; my lips quivered with fear.*

> *My legs gave way beneath me, and I shook in terror.*

I rehearsed the many stories included in this book where I had seen God at work just as Habakkuk had done. At each point I could now see God bigger:

> Bigger than the pain of embracing my loss
> Bigger than the journey to manipulate green in an effort to not hurt.
> Bigger than fighting to be still
> Or ceasing to be angry
> Or living life afraid

Then I began to pray as Habakkuk prayed. (Granted, some of my earlier prayers were not so neat, but this is where I came out.)

Even though I fear that this could happen to me again--this pain of losing again, I still accept and embrace my journey and what it has taught me. (I never thought I would be able to say that!)

Even though I fear that this could happen to me again,
I recognize that You, Lord, were with me through it all. You never left me. You walked with me through the darkest, muddiest, deepest places. It wasn't until I looked back that I could acknowledge you at times, but you were there.

Even though I fear that this could happen to me again
I remember the grace you gave in that moment, Lord.
Grace that you are giving even now to these mothers and their families, Grace that you will give to me again if I need it!

Even though I fear that this could happen to me again
I choose to believe you, to trust you to walk with me through

anything. I open my hands and give to you all that frightens me. I can love and embrace the journey ahead of me.

I can face the future with confidence and trust, joy and enthusiasm
Because I know I am not alone
Because I know that my story will allow me to connect with other mothers
Because I know that You have planted in me a dream
Because I know You have given me skills, abilities and a platform
Because I know that even now You are using my story to impact others
Because I have seen HOPE--and it is contagious!

> *Yet I will rejoice in the Lord!*
> *I will be joyful in the God of my salvation!*
>
> *19 The Sovereign Lord is my strength!*[4]

Getting to the place where I could say these words and mean them was one thing. But once again, that's only half the story. Actually living with open hands was going to be harder than I realized.

Journal Entry:
April 28, 2013

Today she would have been 22,
possibly graduating from college with her friends this May.
Maybe getting married like her other two sisters are this year.

I don't know what she is doing 'right now'!

I sense she is very much alive, thoroughly using the gifts and abilities God has designed her to use, experiencing deeply the joy of being authentically Leisha.

But this morning I sense there is more... much more!

It is dark and I'm aware I am not in my own bed, but in the guest bed at my parent's home. Ren lies beside me sleeping soundly, though he had been so restless the night before. Much like I feel now after waking from a night of dreams.

The dreams were a collage of dreams really--all having a different setting and different characters, too. But the plot was similar.

Somewhere--somehow--something tragic happened and someone died.
Someone was ripped out of the life of another who loved them.
Someone was left with a gaping hole and a horrific ache.

I would stir from one dream only to appear in the middle of

another story with the same heart-wrenching scene.

I lay there sobbing silently--reliving what was my own tragic scene,
Rehashing my own violent emotions,
Longing--deeply longing to hold my girl once again,

To celebrate her birthday with her present--
this day that reminded me she had lived

She had messed up my world from the day she was born
And I knew I would never be the same because of it.

I am eternally grateful.

But this night my heart senses more...much more!

Leisha may not celebrate her 'earth birthday' as much as we do!
I consider the fact that the day she trusted Christ as her Savior might be the day she celebrates.

Or the day she 'ran into heaven' on August 16th.

Maybe that day is of more significance to her now than the day they placed her in my arms and we named her Leisha Danae!

Maybe--because time in heaven is so different than on earth-
Maybe it only feels like seven seconds since she's been there
And not the seven long years I have labored through to find healing.

But there's more!

She is face to face with Jesus, Son of God
Singing, serving, loving, working, welcoming, talking- you know she is talking,

maybe even praying--for me, for her dad and her sisters, for her friends.

I don't know how that works.

The thing that astonished me is that she is 'face to face' with Jesus.

I recall the words of the song
"I can only imagine... what it will be like...when your face...is before me! I can only imagine...when all I will do...is forever... forever worship you. I can only imagine"[1]

As I lay there in the darkness- peace came! The same peace I felt the afternoon I sat with her in the ambulance before they took her away. It was overwhelming peace that everything that was Leisha, except this beautiful shell, had already run on to heaven. The vibrant life I had seen moments before was completely gone.

I knew she was with God now. I never was more sure of anything in my life.

I felt peace! Now- as then!

She is with Jesus!

Safe!

Whole! Not broken!

Kneeling at his feet!

Complete!

I slept!

I woke later in the morning to hear my mom playing the piano as I fondly remember her doing all of my life. My heart was comforted at the sound of it.

Then I realized what she was playing...and I smiled and sang along with the words I could remember....

...face to face, I shall behold him, far beyond the starry sky;

face to face in all his glory, I shall see him (and Leisha) *by and by!*[2]

20 N.E.P.O. Handed

As I pondered the words that would make up this chapter, I reflected back over the journey I have taken since Leisha died. I thumbed through the pages of her journal, and then my own. Page after page filled with thoughts, some random, some ordered, but similar in eerie ways. Both of us shared dreams and stories of special relationships with sisters and friends. I wrote of Rennie and our marriage, she wrote of love yet to come.

Yet they are also filled with emotions and fears that threatened to hold us back from being who God created us to be, more importantly from seeing God in the middle of all that life threw at us. I was in awe of the similarities of thought of a 15 year old daughter and her mom.

One thought struck me more than any other. Over and over as I read through my journal and even the early pages of this book, I noted how many times the Lord had invited me to *open my hands* and release my plans in exchange for his.

- Open my hands where my health was an issue. I struggle with fear of what might yet come, but see the need to take care of myself.

- Open my hands to my daughter's eating disorder. I can't change her, or fix my family, nor do they want me to. But I can do what I need to do to be emotionally, mentally and physically healthy myself. Much of that is a spiritual battle too.

- Open my hands to embrace the shame and guilt that is mine to own, as I experience God's forgiveness and the forgiveness of my girls. Then Open my hands to release it.

- Open my hands to my dream (Chapter 9) and follow the Dream Giver.

Yet I noted that after Leisha died, I never sensed God was asking me to open my hands. Of course, I wasn't always listening either. In fact, I found myself pulling away from my former ways of being in relationship with God. I struggled to read my Bible for a long time. I knew it was God's letter to me, but I didn't want to know what he had to say. My prayer life was filled with angry words. It was one-way conversation at best.

As for church, well, I couldn't seem to get my mind to focus on the message. I only cried through the worship singing. Leisha and I had shared our love of being on the worship team. The worship songs reminded me that the music had been my avenue to sit at the throne. Now when I found myself close, I was deeply aware of the fact that Leisha was near the throne as well. Yet I could not touch her or see her. I ended up coming through the doors of the church primarily because I needed the relationships in the community.

Those disciplines of Bible reading, prayer and church had been a meaningful part of my spiritual walk before. But now I couldn't force myself to go through those same motions. God didn't look the same to me. I knew I would never be the same. How could I ever relate to Him the same way?

Yet I never felt condemned by God for not 'performing' in our relationship as I had before. In fact, as I reflected back on the journals and what I have written in these pages, I noticed that God met me differently. It occurred to me that he broke down the act of opening my hands into smaller baby steps and then led me through each one while he gave me space to move in my own time.

I haven't spoken much of my own childhood, but I looked back on my Life Map and barely recognized the little girl that grew up in a pastor's family and had dreams of one day being special. I was optimistic at heart, but struggled with ever being that girl that would make a real difference in my world.

Nearly 20 years ago, Rennie and I were part of an intense leadership training week with several other couples in a similar stage of life. Our dear friends Art and Deb also participated in this training. As we walked out of one session, Art pointed his finger at me and said, "If you were a color, you would be yellow! Bright, sunny yellow!" You would have thought we had just spent the hour talking about what color we were. We had not! But I was delighted. Then Rennie leaned in and said, "Yeah, she's always pumping sunshine!" I wasn't sure he meant that as a compliment.

But that was me! Yellow! From the time I was a little girl, I wanted to shine with warmth and light, and bring joy to others! I may not have always showed it, but in myself I knew it to be true of me. The colors in my room had been a bright yellow, orange, and green. It struck me that Leisha had painted her room hot yellow, orange and pink and her favorite color was green. I was reminded why I chose the yellow- gold sheet of construction paper at the art therapy session. (Chapter 8)

So what happens when a bright yellow, sunshine-pumping girl comes face to face with the dark places in life and in her soul?

I scrolled through the pages of my life, one significant life-changing event after another, some tragic, but most pretty remarkable. I saw "yellow girl" face each thing, sometimes with tears, but most often with the perspective that good was going to come from this.

- Diagnosed with Addison's,
- Struggle of each of our girls,
- Giving up the role as worship leader,
- Giving up title of pastor's wife.

Each struggle contributed to a loss of confidence in myself, and my ability to care for myself or my girls or my husband, let alone a church full of people that I loved dearly.

But through all of that I still had hope- still pumped sunshine! Yes, this was hard, but all was going to be ok! We were going to be ok! I focused on verses like

Romans 8:28
We know that God causes everything to work together for the good of those who love God and are called according to his purpose for them.[1]

And Jeremiah 29:11
For I know the plans I have for you," says the Lord. "They are plans for good and not for disaster, to give you a future and a hope.[2]

Then a year later on that beautiful August evening, Leisha went for a walk and was hit by car. Everything changed.

I argued with God instead, "I worshiped you, I served you, I was humble, I was loving. How can you let this happen? How can you leave me in this place of brokenness and darkness?"

This bright yellow girl couldn't see any light, only darkness. I for sure couldn't pump enough sunshine to bring light to the dark place, let alone shine a light for others to see. I wasn't sure if the promises of God I had claimed over and over were really true anymore.

Strictly out of obedience I picked up my Bible. I knew enough about God to believe that He would show up in the dark times as he promised he would in the light. And he did! God showed up in the Psalms!

As yellow-sunshine-pumping girl, I had often lingered in the book of Psalms. But I was mostly focused on the praise. Even when things were hard, I looked in the Psalms for how they would lead me to worship.

But now I found myself consumed by the laments. Nearly half of the Psalms contain complaints, or laments, usually directed toward God. The psalmists wrestle with God, cry out to God, weep before God, and even blame God for misery and suffering. Even though they believed that God was great, they also saw him as gracious enough to absorb the rawness of their emotion. They believed he was strong enough to withstand the hostility we pour on him.

The Psalms helped me put my emotions into words. They taught me to be honest when I spoke to God. The psalmists spoke truth about their circumstances, especially about their feelings. Unfortunately, somewhere along the line many of us grew up with the message that we can be honest, but don't be too honest. People can't always handle it. We transfer that to God too!

But God doesn't seem to take offense to our complaints. If anything, he invites our honest expression. Psalm 51:6 tells us, *"You desire honesty from the heart so you can teach us to be wise in our inmost being."* [3]

It took quite a while for me to dare to trust that God wouldn't strike me with lightning if I told him how I really felt about things. The fact that he, being God, already knew these things didn't seem to sway me. But if I am not being honest, chances are I am not being open either.

How do I open my hands when I am no longer 'yellow girl', but rather filled with anger and fears? I am in the fighter stance ready to swing at anything that is in my way like the woman in Nouwen's story of the last chapter.

I remember the day I turned to Psalm 77 in my Praise and Worship Bible that I have used at my bedside for years. The page was marked up with notes and underlining. I knew it well, especially verses 11 and 12 which stood out for me in the teaching of my mentor and friend, Linda Dillow, years earlier.

As I look back on that time, I have noticed that the Psalm led me to the baby steps that God invited me to take when I couldn't open my hands like I had before. The psalmist showed me how.

- **First he taught me to NOTICE:**

I cry out to God; yes, I shout.
   Oh, that God would listen to me!
2 When I was in deep trouble,
   I searched for the Lord.
All night long I prayed, with hands lifted toward heaven,
   but my soul was not comforted.
3 I think of God, and I moan,
   overwhelmed with longing for his help. Interlude
4 You don't let me sleep.
   I am too distressed even to pray!

₅ I think of the good old days,
  long since ended,
₆ when my nights were filled with joyful songs.
  I search my soul and ponder the difference now.⁴

These verses could have been pulled directly from my journal. I resonated with every word. I noticed how I was feeling now. I couldn't sleep. I was too distressed to pray. The good old days were filled with yellow days when I could sing from a joyful heart. But they were gone now and the next few verses choked my heart now as I had to come to terms with the next step.

- **I had to EXPRESS honestly how I felt especially about God:**

₇ Has the Lord rejected me forever?
  Will he never again be kind to me?
₈ Is his unfailing love gone forever?
  Have his promises permanently failed?
₉ Has God forgotten to be gracious?
  Has he slammed the door on his compassion?
  And I said, "This is my fate;
  the Most High has turned his hand against me."⁵

Sometimes I felt ashamed of telling God how I really felt, I was embarrassed, guilty and even disrespectful. There were many times I wouldn't let myself honestly say what I was feeling about God. My daughters would say things that expressed their questions about why God would allow these things to happen. "I believe God is who you've said he is- so why would he do this to us?" Or "How can you serve a God that would let something like this happen?"

I understood that! At first I chalked it up to their experience with God as still new. They haven't 'learned' what I've learned. But in all my 'learnedness', I was deeply troubled!

I did and do believe God is who he says he is.
I do believe that he is the Blessed Controller who sees all and knows all.
I do believe that Satan is alive and active in our world- but God is greater!

So... if I'm honest, ultimately my struggle is... I believe God is responsible for Leisha's death. Whoa! Did I just write that out loud?

Is he the Blessed Controller of ALL Things?
I believe he is!

Could he have intervened?
Yes!

Does he or does he not have the power to raise up Leisha?
He DOES!

THEN WHY DIDN'T HE?

How could <u>MY GOD</u> allow this to happen to me?

That was me being honest. After all this time, I don't know why. I may never know why! At this stage, I still have more questions than I have answers. But I don't believe for one millisecond he lost control of what was happening. Yet I did feel like the psalmist.

Where are you God?
Where is your mercy?

Lovely Traces of Hope

Have you forgotten to be kind?
Where are your answers?
Why don't you say something??????

I've come to recognize that the greatest tragedy in my story was that at my moment of greatest need, I lost confidence in my God!

Our family had gone through such hard times, we had 'done the hard stuff' to find ways to heal. The girls were just really 'blooming' each in their own way, especially Leisha! We were seeing wholeness in so many ways!

WHY THIS, LORD? WHY NOW? IT'S NOT RIGHT!!!!!

Jerry Sittser, was deeply honest about it, yet in the end, he found God to be 'big enough' for all of it. He writes,

> *"rightly or wrongly, I challenged the integrity of God's character, calling him a bully and a brute. As I look back now, I realize that I was probably wrong to charge God so ruthlessly. Yet I was so distraught, angry and confused that I had to do something with my emotions. I decided to pour it out to God. 'I would never treat anyone like you are treating me.' 'Pick on someone your own size. Leave me alone.' 'I want nothing to do with you."[6]*

Asaph got it too! His bottom line comes in verse 10, "This is my fate; *the Most High has turned his hand against me.*" (Actually it is more like, *"Woe is me"* with the back of hand to the forehead!!) Sometimes in our sophisticated religiosity, we say that kind of thing. We take pride in our pious sayings and martyred attitudes.

Or maybe that's why we can't say it. I tried hard to say what I SHOULD say as a 'good Christian.' I thought I was modeling a gracious spirit. But actually I was denying the depth of my anguish and in many ways making excuses for God, as if he needed me to. It only made him weak and powerless in my eyes. It only added to the loss of my confidence in him.

Sittser reminded me that *"The Psalms invites us to channel our emotions toward God and turn them into a prayer, so that in the end our emotions enrich our relationship with God. "* He goes on to say, *"That we pray honestly, whether expressing praise or rage, prayer does accomplish at least one thing. It pushes us toward God."*[7]

Surprisingly as we look through scripture, God seems to look with compassion and favor on those who accuse him or yell at him. At least they are being honest! What God can't tolerate is a plastic saint, a polite believer, someone who plays a part but never gets into the soul of the character he or she plays.

And rather than God appearing weak or incompetent, someone hardly worth taking seriously, we begin to see him as big enough to absorb our accusations and to take full responsibility for the suffering in the world. The Psalms put God squarely at the center of the problem. God is good, sovereign, and wise, responsible for running the universe. Exactly where He's supposed to be!

I would rather see him as God in the middle of reality--different than I expected but bigger than I have ever known him to be- than doubt if he's big enough in my 'nice' facade.

I know it can be frightening to be that transparent. I remember envisioning myself sitting on God's lap and not mincing any words. In fact, one particularly bad day, I stomped his toes and beat on his chest until I couldn't beat any more.

Exhausted and poured out at the end of the wrestling, where was

I? I was in his arms sobbing with the little breath left in me. It was a moment of deepest intimacy that I will never forget.

That was when the verses 11 and 12 took on a much deeper meaning and turned things around.

- **They created a PIVOT: a perspective change.**

I will remember the deeds of the Lord;
  yes, I will recall your miracles of long ago.
12 I will consider all your works
  and meditate on all your mighty deeds."[8]

It appears nothing changed for Asaph except for his choice to turn from the circumstances he was experiencing to see God. In that moment of crisis, he turns from all that he has **noticed**, and **expressed honestly** to God and he chooses to **pivot**. In the middle of the pain, he made three intentional choices.

- I will remember
- I will recall
- I will consider and meditate.

It made me think of Leisha's *intentional list* hanging on the back of her bedroom door. Each line started with **I will.** Each phrase indicated the behavior she wanted to be true of her. She had identified the choices she wanted to make as she lived life even when circumstances surprised her.

Linda Dillow paraphrased this verse this way in her book *The Blessing Book.* "*Today all is dark. I can't see what God is doing, but instead of staying here and letting the problems paralyze me, **I will** turn my mind to what God has done in the past.*[9] (Blessings, pg. 32) Linda speaks of an intentional choice she made ahead of time so she knew how she wanted to behave when it was hard to think it through.

The words in the margin of my Bible said April 1994 I WILL! Ten years before Leisha died, I made a decision to turn my mind from the problems to remember the incredible ways God has worked in my own past.

My next words were just as the psalmists!

- **O God:**

O God, your ways are holy.
   Is there any god as mighty as you?
14 You are the God of great wonders!
   You demonstrate your awesome power among the nations.
15 By your strong arm, you redeemed your people,
   the descendants of Jacob and Joseph. Interlude

16 When the Red Sea saw you, O God,
   its waters looked and trembled!
   The sea quaked to its very depths.
17 The clouds poured down rain;
   the thunder rumbled in the sky.
   Your arrows of lightning flashed.
18 Your thunder roared from the whirlwind;
   the lightning lit up the world!
   The earth trembled and shook.[10]

I recalled the day Leisha died. All I could say at that country corner was "O". Days later my prayer became, "O God", over and over! Then I became consumed with the pain and the darkness of the grief tunnel. My prayer turned to anger over the loss and what I was feeling.

The psalmist continues...When the Red Sea saw you O GOD...

19 *Your road led through the sea,*

your pathway through the mighty waters—

a pathway no one knew was there!

20 *You led your people along that road like a flock of sheep,*

with Moses and Aaron as their shepherds. [10]

There it was! The way through the grief tunnel! I couldn't imagine I would ever find it, but leaning into the darkness and embracing what was my reality, God met me! Each step became another time for me to say yes to his next baby step. Each time there was another sliver of green to point me in the right direction to the path.

When I was ready,
When I made the effort to notice,
When I dared to express honestly all the emotions
When I intentionally chose to pivot
I saw God!

Always present!
Through all the muck and the mire of the tunnel, he had never left my side!
Through all my anger and lashing out, he had always stayed by me!
Through the darkness, he kept me on the path.

I looked down at my hands. They weren't closed in a fist any longer. They were open!

The Lord had taught me to take baby steps to:
> N: Notice
> E: Express Honestly
> P: Pivot Intentionally
> O: O God!

N.E.P.O.! That's OPEN backwards! God never asked me to open my hands after Leisha died. But he taught me how to do it one tiny step at a time. In my journey with the Lord, I've learned two things:

1. An OPEN HANDED life is much richer than one with closed fists.
2. To keep my nails short in case I forget.

What can we do if our hands are open?
- We can receive something.
- We can welcome our toddler.
- We can cheer on our soccer player or a teammate at work.
- We can celebrate.
- We can shake the hand of another.
- We can reach out to help someone.
- We can pray, folding hands together or keeping them open and to receive.
- We can praise, lifting his name higher with raised arms and open hands.

Nowhere in the tunnel had he asked me to open my hands to him as he had many times before. But instead he led me, one step at a time to a place of safety and trust; to a place where I could see him and find the path through the tunnel.

I was led to worship again from a joyous, and yes, bright yellow heart. I had to go through green hope to get there, but I have rejoiced that I feel some yellow once again.

Henry Nouwen shared a quote from one of his students, *"I see hope as an attitude where everything stays open before me. Not that I don't think of my future in those moments, but I think of it in an entirely different way. Daring to stay open to whatever will come to me today, tomorrow, two months from now, or a year from now--that is hope. To go FEARLESSLY into things without knowing how they'll turn out, to keep on going, even when something doesn't work the first time, to have trust in whatever you're doing- that is living with hope."*[11]

Journal Entry:
January 30, 2016

I sat in my living room with my friend Beth one recent January day. The power of the moment was evident from her very first words. Powerful because I understood in an intimate way by what I was experiencing myself. The last weeks were hard. It felt as if life as we hoped it would be was not possible; heaven couldn't come soon enough.

As we shared, we began to find more connections of our stories. Sadness was evident even though we both expressed that we were feeling better today.

I asked, "What are you grieving?"

She was thinking hard as we prepared our cups of honey and ginseng tea with tea bags she brought from home. As we sat down at the table, she pulled out a notecard she had already been working on.

"These are a list of the stresses in my life. Is this perhaps what I am grieving?"

She shared her list. I nodded my head with acknowledgment. Yes! Her list could be mine. There were variations on a theme, but we each shared emotions wrapped around

- Family
- Losses of loved ones

- Business as entrepreneurs
- Dreams
- Book projects
- And all the other things we wanted to do because of our business, dreams and book projects.

At times when she spoke, her countenance was downcast and broken. At other times her spirit soared and it was evident in the way she expressed her plans.

Should I quit? Am I just supposed to start something for someone else to finish?

I shook my head NO! It wasn't because I had prayed about it or had confirmation from the Lord. I hadn't and I didn't! But she did! Everything she talked about was full of vibrancy. My gut instinct told me she was really close and knew what she wanted to see happen.

She was just really tired. She couldn't see her next step.

Mixed in other questions and comments, she casually asked the question, "Why do I have to fill so many holes?" The words caught my attention.

Why do we try so hard to fill all these holes we have in our heart?

Will you ever be able to fill the hole that Tim left? No!

I knew I couldn't fill the hole Leisha left in my heart.

At the same time, we leaned in close to each other and whispered, "I wouldn't want to!"
We sat back and stared at each other!

Truth! We wouldn't want to fill the holes and try to make it as if our loved ones were never there. We're trying to fill the holes disappointment had left. We are working to close the holes left by losses and heartbreak.

But in reality, the holes remind us that her husband Tim and my daughter Leisha lived. They had made a tremendous difference in our lives. We would never want to eliminate that even if it meant feeling the ache for years after.

"It is our holes that make us holy!" I pondered out loud.

"Yes," she said, "the holes in our heart reflect his glory with more radiance than if our heart were whole."

I went to the kitchen and brought back a ceramic bowl. I held it at the bottom and explained that I got this bowl because I thought it would be the perfect size cereal bowl for Rennie. But when I got it home, I looked inside and noticed it was punched full of holes. It was not a cereal bowl, it was a colander. The holes gave it a different purpose.

Again we stared at each other. The holes in our heart had given us a different purpose in life as well. We were not the same people any more. I suddenly wondered about Lazarus. How did being in the grave change him? After Jesus raised him from the dead, could he be as he was before? Surely being brought to life literally had some of the same effects it was having on me since I had come through the grief tunnel.

I saw people and circumstances with different eyes.
I heard dreams and heart cries with greater understanding.
I tasted life and love with deeper appreciation.

But did Lazarus still feel the holes of his heart? Or were they healed too? Mine weren't. In fact, since the time I was aware I was not in the grief tunnel anymore, I became more aware of the holes that were still there.

Leisha, yes of course! She was the gaping, jagged hole that nearly left me dead.
But there was the pain of leaving the pastorate.
There was the ache for my daughters.
There was the consequence of my health.

Each one left a hole in my heart that remains to this day. Yet they also remind me of a sweet time, of a preciousness of relationships and growth. They were times when the nearness of the Lord was so evident and so cherished. I never want to forget that!

So why do I keep trying to fill the holes? How do I keep living with them?

Beth continued to review with me some of the 'holes' she was grieving. Her thoughts turned to a time long ago--a moment when life mixed with loss. Her eyes filled with tears and my heart felt her pain. The tears began to spill out from a place so deep, so buried, we knew we were on sacred ground.

This is it! This is the reason she couldn't go on. She needed to acknowledge how this particular pain is impacting her future. Again I understood. I was beginning to reconnect with my own forgotten grief.

That hole had become clogged. It was keeping us from doing what we were to do next. I have been amazed how quickly I could go from seeing all the possibilities to having no hope. Just that fast I saw darkness, thought toxic thoughts, and spoke explosive words. I was angry and fearful of all the holes in my heart from past losses and hurts.

But the TRUTH IS the holes in my life have been part of me becoming holy! I have seen God show up, not to fill the holes, but to radiate through them.

The holes make us holy!

The tears subsided. We took a deep breath. We prayed for one another. We hugged each other good bye.

We came as broken people, shared from the broken places and left as broken people. But we were whole--made holy by a Savior who had holes in his own hand so that we could endure the holes in our life.

The holes make us holy!

> *For God, who said, "Let there be light in the darkness," has made this light shine in our hearts so we could know the glory of God that is seen in the face of Jesus Christ.*
>
> *7 We now have this light shining in our hearts, but we ourselves are like fragile clay jars containing this great treasure. This makes it clear that our great power is from God, not from ourselves.*
>
> *8 We are pressed on every side by troubles, but we are not crushed. We are perplexed, but not driven to despair. 9 We are hunted down, but never abandoned by God. We get knocked down, but we are not destroyed. 10 Through suffering, our bodies continue to share in the death of Jesus so that the life of Jesus may also be seen in our bodies.*
>
> 2 Corinthians 4:6-10[1]

21 Faith, Hope and Love

My dear reader,

The fact that you have read through this book to reach this chapter means that you have shared life with me.

I do not want to just tell you my story and leave you there. I want for my story to connect with your story. Most likely your story includes loss, though it is different than mine. I want to be a voice that reminds you that the loss does not need to define you. I hope you will take advantage of the questions I have included in the *Tracing Your Own Story* section that follows. Consider that if my story has influenced you in some way, your story has that potential as well. I also have other resources available on my author page that might be of help to you. Be sure to check them out at www.kathyburrus.com.

This may be the final chapter of *Lovely Traces of Hope,* but the story is not over. Leisha's life here on earth is finished, yet the influence of her story continues. In the *Epilogue,* you will find some of the ways her friends and family continue to share that influence through their own unique personalities and opportunities.

This is not fiction. These are real life stories about people who sometimes get it right and sometimes not! I can't just make something up about how *"they live happily ever after"* because

ACT 3 remains to be seen. It depends greatly on how we choose to respond to all that life brings to us.

In the telling of my story here, I have come to understand some important truths that I may or may not have made clear as I wrote these chapters. In the middle of the journey, particularly Leisha's death, I thought that making the decision to see hope – to notice the slivers of green--had been the secret of finding my way out of the grief tunnel. As I pulled back from these chapters I have already written, I got a glimpse of something bigger! Something I knew again as if for the first time!

Seeing hope involves Faith--Hope--and Love. These are not steps we take, but rather more like a river that naturally flows in and out of each which leads us to LIFE.

Take a look!

1. **FAITH is our foundation. Faith is where we gain the stability to reflect on our past. Faith gives us perspective.**

When I mention the word faith, we might each come up with a different definition of what faith is. One person might think of their connection with a particular religious group or church. Another might say it is a 'feeling' or mystical experience of some sort.

Still others might think of it as *'believing hard"* like the little engine that said "I think I can, I think I can, I think I can". But just believing doesn't do anything. What's most important is what or who we believe in.

"If there is no object of our faith, it's just faith in faith, or faith in our emotions, or faith in our experiences....Biblical faith believes in a very specific God with a very specific character

and plan." (Chip Ingram, Holy Ambition, pg. 93)[1]

The Bible gives us a great definition of faith.

Hebrews 11:1 says, *Faith shows the reality of what we hope for; it is the evidence of things we cannot see.*[2]

Verse 6 goes on to say that *it is impossible to please God without faith. Anyone who wants to come to him must believe that God exists and that he rewards those who sincerely seek him.*[2]

I don't know what your relationship is with Jesus Christ. I don't know how you feel about God or the Bible at this point in your life. I know for many of us, Scripture has become lifeless and church has become a judgement hall. I know that our perspective has come from our journey through 'religiosity' sometimes, rather than a personal relationship with the LIVING ONE WHO DIED.

That changes things! Often life happens to us in tragic, painful ways and we can't imagine how God, being God, (Father, Son, and Holy Spirit) could allow those kinds of things to happen to people-any people! So sometimes that keeps our faith from being real, it keeps our faith limited because we don't trust God!

And yet many times, we have just enough faith. Scripture teaches about having the faith of a mustard seed (Matthew 17:20). Sometimes we have just enough faith to believe that HE IS! Sometimes that is all we need- enough faith to believe that *"Living One died and now lives forever and ever!"* (Revelation 1:18)[3] There is the truth!

I grew up going to church. My dad was the pastor, and our family of seven lived across the driveway from our church. So often, not only did I attend every service that ever was, but I probably helped clean the week before, straighten the class rooms and turn on the lights before our church family came.

I grew up having Sunday night sword drills and participating in scripture memory challenges learning over 100 verses at one time. Of course the guy I was 'competing' with had learned almost 700. Oh well!

I had trusted Jesus Christ, the Living One who died, as my Savior when I was 7. I committed my life to full time ministry of some kind when I was 13 and shortly after was baptized.

I went to Bible College and had a double major in Bible and Church Music.

I had been a Pastor's wife, and a worship leader, but mostly a worshiper.

I had pointed people to see the Lord. I had prayed for them; I had read scripture over them.

But after Leisha died, I really distanced myself from God. I was full of questions and aware that God must be very different than I thought he was for this to be part of his plan.

I prayed, but it was not like before. I didn't have any order to my prayer life or intentionally bring up the names of all those I loved. I prayed for me! I prayed for Rennie, Caitlin and Brielle. I prayed for Leisha's grandparents. I prayed for Abby and others who were impacted by her death. Beyond those people, I probably didn't pray for others!

I started reading the Bible that morning after she died. But as my grief intensified, I began to withdraw from the book; except for the Psalms. For some reason the psalmists almost always said it like it was. They gave hope because after remembering all that was wrong with the world, their faith was their foundation. They remembered who God was, and how he had showed up in the past.

And it was those Bible stories I had learned as a small child that came to mind again and again to remind me of the many ways God worked in the lives of ordinary people. It caused me to see the different ways he showed himself so that people would see him. That made all the difference.

My faith was strengthened by my own back story because it was full of instances where God had shown up, intimately!

- Miss Lipscomb--the power of prayer, God's intimate involvement with a teenager
- Leisha's birth story--baby Eric
- Leisha's name--take Leesha's place

Each of these places, and many more beside, taught me that God was paying attention to me. I had to trust that he was here now too, in Leisha's death. He cared for me. He was intimately acquainted with my grief.

All that had been part of my faith journey until now was reminding me to trust again. Any box I had created about who God was and how he should behave had been crushed. But God was still God. He was still good. He was still right. He was still in control.

So when the Living One invited me to *Turn East* (chapter 13), I believed enough to say yes! As I renewed my faith to believe that GOD IS, I dared to look for hope!

2. HOPE is the confident expectation of our faith. Hope is where we find the courage to take the risk and focus on our future. Hope gives us purpose.

Some people use hope as a synonym for a wish or desire; they hope they get the job, or make the grades, or have all their dreams come to pass. But in the bible, hope is not a wish, but a reality; a fact not yet realized.

Hope causes us to look confidently into the future because we have faith in God's character and plan, even if we struggle with the circumstances and situations in life. Hope motivates us to courageously take next steps.

My faith gave me the ability to hope:
- the night of the accident,
- In Leisha's words and reminders
- the weekend of the memorial service,
- And at the country corner when I turned east.

In whatever grief tunnel or the dark place you are in, there is hope that there is something more, something better ahead. Because we have some faith, we dare to notice hope--it may be slivers of Green Hope, but we look for it. We start to pay attention to the kairos in any given moment and admit this is not a random experience.

We take the next breath, we close our eyes to see, and we dare to be still so we can notice where the LIVING ONE breaks into our world even now echoing the words,
    I love you!
    I will not leave you!
    I will carry you!

When we have hope, when hope comes to fulfillment, then we can begin to look outside of ourselves. Probably not until then! We may be pretty self-focused when we are so needy ourselves. Notice I did not say 'self-centered'! There is a tremendous difference! When we are experiencing this level of pain, often we reach out to others in an effort to find relief, or to get something from them to ease the hurt. Our friends know they can't meet those needs so they distance themselves from us. We too often feel like they have let us down so we tune them out of our lives. Then it feels like we are being self- centered.

But when we are self-focused, we are intentional about listening to our own heart, our own needs, our own heart cries! God is speaking to us in the middle of all the noise of chaos and pain. It is all we can do to take care of ourselves and those closest to us at the time. Often we must give ourselves permission to do just that; even as we are gracious with those who struggle to let us do that.

When we begin to see hope fulfilled, we can begin to focus outside of ourselves in an authentic, loving way which leads us to Love! Faith, Hope and Love! Scripture teaches us that Love is the greatest gift. I get that more than I ever have before.

   3. LOVE frees us to encounter the presence of God and others in our life and allows us to engage in the present. Loves gives us passion!

Because of the hope, I was able to open my hands to God and to others and allow the mess, the real of life, to show me the beauty of love. As I did I was able to reach out to others. Grief sometimes causes us to hide away in the 'self-focused' times I spoke of earlier.

Over time, I had a restored desire for relationships, especially in the community of my church. I engaged in my new career role as a life coach, and was able to genuinely care for the needs and goals of my clients. I invested in family and friends and instead of being in desperate need of what they could do for me; I was able to speak into the needs of their lives as well.

These relationships reached deep into my core and lifted me to new places as a woman, a wife, a mom, a friend, a sister or daughter. Each person shared life giving companionship in their own way.

That leads us to LIFE!

4. **When we have faith that has pointed us to hope, and hope releases us to love, then we experience LIFE!**

We experience life as it was meant to be, abundant and full. No, not perfect. But there is a goodness, a fullness, and a richness to it that we may not have had otherwise.

Scripture reminds us of the LIVING ONE who described himself as *I am the resurrection and the life.*[4] He calls us out of the darkness and invites us to take off the grave clothes and breathe Life. (John 11) Again, no, it's not a perfect life but it can be good!

The morning I stood on that worship stage and felt the breeze of Life blowing against my face, (Chapter 18) my hands were open in worship.

- With open hands I could dare to notice where the Living One showed up in my past because I had faith that God is worthy of my trust.
- With open hands I could confidently expect that God would show up in my future.
- With open hands I could begin to reach out and touch the lives of others in my present world with greater care and passion than ever before!

It is with open hands that I

Became a life, marriage and grief coach.

Work with women who long to embrace their whole story.

Am writing you now!

I so wish Leisha could have written the end of this book just as she wrote the first chapter. In many ways, she did through the Lovely Traces she left for me to find.

Yet the story really isn't about Leisha, or about me! It is about the Living One who died and showed up in our story over and over again. It is in the middle of the darkness, in the mess of it all, that we can see God, bigger, different and more than enough. Sometimes we have to close our physical eyes and open the eyes of our heart. We have to look for him, not as we think we know him, or as we expect him to be. But we must notice him for the myriad of ways he keeps showing up!

If you do not know the Living One who died, or if you have questions about your relationship with him, please stop by www.kathyburrus.com and send me an email. Sometimes we need someone else to hold a mirror for us to see God in our own story.

He's there! I've seen him! And yes! He is big enough!
Here is to living a hopeful, open handed, courageous life.

> Engage your faith, little as it seems, and become a see-er of hope.

> Embrace your hope, even if it is only slivers of green, and become a pointer to hope.

> Empower your hope as you share your story out of love, and become a life-giving influence to your world.

Leisha's lovely traces left me with the words "I want to influence! I want to say I'm going, come with me!"

Well, I'm going! Will you come with me?

What lovely traces will you leave behind?

Leisha's mom,
Kathy

May the God of Green Hope
fill you up with joy,
fill you up with peace,
so that your believing lives,
filled with the life-changing energy of the Holy Spirit,
will brim over with hope!
Romans 15:13[5]

Legacy-- Nicole Nordeman

I choose to include this song here, because this was on the CD Leisha was listening to on her walk the afternoon of her death. We spoke about it briefly in those short moments I had with her on the road way. The words continue to inspire me as they had her.

From Nicole's Woven and Spun Album

I don't mind if you've got something nice to say about me
And I enjoy an accolade like the rest
And you could take my picture and hang it in a gallery
Of all the who's who and so-and-so
That used to be the best at such and such
It wouldn't matter much
I won't lie, it feels alright to see your name in lights
We all need an 'Atta Boy' or 'Atta Girl'
In the end I'd like to hang my hat on more besides
The temporary trappings of this world

I want to leave a legacy, how will they remember me?
Did I choose to love? Did I point to you enough
To make a mark on things? I want to leave an offering
A child of mercy and grace who blessed your name
Unapologetically and leave that kind of legacy

I don't have to look too far or too long awhile
To make a lengthy list of all that I enjoy
It's an accumulating trinket and a treasure pile
Where moth and rust, thieves and such will soon enough destroy

Not well traveled, not well read
Not well-to-do or well-bred
I just want to hear instead
"Well done good and faithful one"

I want to leave a legacy, how will they remember me?
Did I choose to love? Did I point to you enough
To make a mark on things? I want to leave an offering
A child of mercy and grace who blessed your name
Unapologetically and leave that kind of legacy[6]

Songwriter: Nichole Nordeman
Publisher: ARIOSE MUSIC © 2009 by Gracenote. All rights reserved.
Used with permission.

Tracing Hope in Your Own Story

By Kathy Burrus
And YOU!

For more information or resources,
Go to kathyburrus.com

Tracing Hope in Your Own Story

Listening to someone else's story can have a tremendous influence on us. We can walk away from the story teller or put down the book and be grateful for that moment of sharing that has moved us in a powerful way.

You may have read *Lovely Traces of Hope* because there is something you want from my story to help you with yours. I understand you might have experienced a loss or a hurt that is so painful. I am so sorry for the pain you feel or fear.

But the sharing of our stories is meant to do more than strike a chord or inspire us to feel good.

- What if my story was meant to connect you to the part of your own story that begs to be noticed and heard?

- What if each of us listened to our own story? Listened for the beauty and the power of our own hopes and dreams, fears and pain, and the lessons they teach us.

In *Lovely Traces of Hope*, Leisha showed me the power of her story and reminded me that I needed to pay attention to my own. I'm here to do the same for you!

I've included a few questions to get you started as you begin to listen in a new way to your story. Use the ones that are useful to you, leave the others for another time. If you would like to delve more deeply into your story, there are additional resources that are available to help you do that at <u>kathyburrus.com</u>.

Using references to lessons I have shared in the *Lovely Traces of Hope,* you will find other questions, exercises, even activities that invite you to ponder, write, and even play with your story.

I hope you will take some time to sit with the wonderful story of you and all that it has to teach you about life and love, your design and your purpose.

Most importantly, it can show you throughout the high points and the hard times of your journey, the fingerprints of an ever present God. How has the *Living One who died* shown up for you? What is the message he brought for you when he did?

That is a story worth listening too!

> *Listen to your life. See it for fathomless mystery that it is.*
> *In the boredom and pain of it*
> *no less in the excitement and gladness:*
> *Touch, taste, smell your way to the holy and hidden part of it,*
> *Because in the last analysis, all moments are key moments,*
> *And life itself is grace.*
> ~Frederick Buechner[1]

Title of Your Story

The title of my book, *Lovely Traces of Hope,* was decided by my daughter Leisha. As far as I could tell from her journal, she found the words *Lovely Traces* in a song that resonated with her by the same name.

I added the *of Hope* to the title because the lovely traces Leisha left for me all pointed me to hope; green hope, life giving hope. For me, it was a most appropriate way to describe all that Leisha had left for me to find my way through my grief.

Titles are an important part of any work because it is invitation to the reader to engage with the story. The title needs to represent what the story is about, but it also must draw in the reader to engage with the story.

As you consider all that has been your journey, what would the title of your story be?

Stories of Your Life

I encourage you to set aside space today to just notice! Take some time to ponder the journey your life has taken. Your story has so much to tell you.

Our life is filled with stories; many seem random, some have been forgotten, some are merely memories that have a sentiment to us still as we ponder them. But then there are the ones that we can remember with great detail because they significantly transformed us. So what are the stories in your own life that changed the way you thought about everything?

What does your early life story look like?

What was significant during your high school years? College years?

What stands out in terms of jobs or opportunities that you have experienced since then?

Who are the heroes in your story? Or the un-heroes?

What kind of conversation would you like to have with them?

What are some ways these stories continue to impact your current relationships?

For more help in identifying what your story is telling you or information about life-mapping go to
www.kathyburrus.com.

Pivot Points from the Past

Choose one of the stories that you have already indicated has been significant. Maybe it was something you did, or witnessed, or were part of because of the circumstances you found yourself in.

When you think about that moment, what do you remember?

Who was there? Who wasn't there?

What were your emotions?

What did you do because of those emotions?

What is the message that is still tied to that memory?

How is that message continuing to influence your attitudes and decisions in current situations?

What's Your Response?

Take a look at some of the stories and pivot points you have identified in the last few exercises.

What was your response to these events?

What was the outcome based on your response?

What are you learning from the responses, outcomes and messages you have identified?

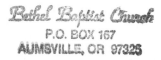

Embracing the Pain

Again, take a look at the transformational, significant events of your story. Consider looking deeply into the emotions of one of the greatest pains.

What do you sense the LIVING ONE is asking you to do with this pain?

Is there a point you may need to consider 'turning east' and walking into the darkness rather than trying to run from it? How would it change you to find hope in that moment rather than just loss?

How does your relationship with the Jesus affect your ability to turn east or embrace the loss?

If you are struggling with this section, please seek out a trusted friend or counselor. While it feels like we are alone in this journey, it is often healing to have someone walking with us as we take this important step to move forward from our grief.

Celebrating the Green!

What color is your hope?

Where is the Living One who Died showing up in your story?

What is your RED SEA story; the story in your life that you find yourself retelling over and over that reminds you to hope?

Who are the people in your world waiting to be influenced by your story?

What lovely traces will you leave behind?

Where are you in the journey? We would love to hear your story. Please stop by <u>kathyburrus.com</u> and share with us what you have learned from the *Lovely Traces* of your own story.

Epilogue

Artwork by Brielle Burrus Augsburger,
Once Upon A Summertime, 2006 Used with Permission.

It felt important to acknowledge how Leisha's HOPE is continuing to influence others to hope! So we chose to include some of the stories of influence from her friends and family. These are just a few we know of. If you would like to share your story too, go to <u>kathyburrus.com</u> and share your journey to hope.

Abby Dean

I am most often asked how Abby is doing, the friend that witnessed Leisha's accident. I thought I would let her tell you in her own words.

Leisha was one of my fun friends. While there were seasons of life where we would see each other on a regular basis, that wasn't always the case. When we did get together though, we were always able to pick up right where we left off. Sometimes I thought Leisha was over the top and wore way too much mascara. But we always had fun together, laughing and being silly.

I loved that Leisha lived life her way, she did her makeup and her hair how she wanted and she wore what she wanted and didn't care what other people thought about it. If she wanted to eat a huge spoonful of frosting, then she ate a huge spoonful of frosting. She lived unashamed, bold in her faith, bold in her love.

One of my greatest struggles after the accident was with knowing how to handle the grieving process. Journaling was something I did a lot and still do to this day that helps me process things and pour my heart out to God. I also found music to be very therapeutic, as was just spending time with people who loved me and cared about me.

I don't ever recall feeling angry. I guess with God's help I made peace with the situation. Peace that I couldn't change it. It happened for a reason and Leisha is up in Heaven having a ball. One of my most vivid memories of Leisha is one night we were at my house, outside laying on the lawn looking up at the stars. It was shortly after her family left St. John and she was just pouring her heart out about her struggles and how rough life had been for her. Trial after trial she was frustrated and disgusted. Not that death is ever the answer for the trails we go through, and I know that her death has brought about pain and sorrow for many. But sometimes I can't help but be happy for her and maybe even a little jealous!! It brings me comfort to know that she is in a place of bliss and rejoicing. I guess one of the biggest things I have to be thankful for in this whole situation is that my friend did without a doubt know the Lord and her eternity is being spent in Heaven. Our life here is but a breath and I know that one day soon I will see her again!

Every day I do my best to be grateful for life, be grateful for the things God has blessed me with and the breath in my lungs. Life is a gift.

Sarah Smith

In short, Leisha was my best friend. I do not know if I was among her best friends but that does not matter. She was mine. Let me explain how that happened.

I joined the Ohio HEAT Lady Eagles basketball team when I was 11-years-old. Leisha did not play that year but she hung out with the team all the time. I honestly had not had a ton of interaction with girls my own age before, most of the ones I would hang out with at that time were younger than me by three years or more. The rest of my time with social interactions was spent with my three brothers and their friends. I joined the team to meet other homeschool girls my age and build friendships.

At first I did not feel like I fit in. I did not care much about fashion or make-up and cared little about boys, and these were the main topics talked about in the girls' locker room. None of the girls asked me to hang out before or after practice while the younger and older siblings had practice. Instead I sat by myself working on school work.

I started feeling like something was wrong with me and like the other girls did not like me because I was overweight, did not care about the things they cared about, and generally wasn't pretty. It was the first time in my life I compared myself to other girls and I really felt like I was garbage. As a result of all of this I stopped eating and pushed myself on the court to try to lose weight and earn favor with the girls on my team. I know this was incredibly stupid but at the time it made sense.

Leisha noticed. My little plan had only been in effect for 2 weeks but that was enough for Leisha to tell that something was wrong. She pulled me aside after practice one day, looked me dead in the eye and said, *"You don't even know that you are beautiful do you? God created you and saying there is something about yourself you want to change is telling him that he messed up, and he doesn't make mistakes."*

I will never forget that conversation as long as I live. Up until that point the only people who had ever told me that I was beautiful were my family members. She was the first person who was not genetically obligated to make me feel wanted, beautiful, and special to do so for me; something I thanked her for a couple of years later during a heart-to-heart before basketball practice.

Our friendship grew and time and time again Leisha proved that she genuinely loved me and cared about me and wanted to be a part of my life. Words do not express what her friendship meant to me. I can never thank her enough for seeing me in that dark moment, and speaking truth and life to me that would change my life. So whether or not the deep love and appreciation was mutual or not, Leisha was my best friend.

I remember the first time that someone told me that my story mattered, that God was using it, that Leisha's life mattered, and that I was part of the legacy she left behind. I was 17-years-old and was assigned the task of giving my testimony at Teens For Christ. A week later one of the leaders in my chapter came up to me and said how she and her husband had recently had dinner at the Burrus house and of course Leisha was talked about. I do not know the details of the dinner but I know that this leader was so impacted that she felt the need to tell me, *"You sharing your story of Leisha is keeping her alive in ways you don't understand. You are a part of God's bigger plan with all of this. He is going to use this in your life and in the lives of others. Don't stop telling your story."*

And so I just want to say the same to you, Kathy, and anyone else who is a part of Leisha's Legacy. Don't stop telling your story.

Kristen Bergmaier, cousin

I feel like I was really getting closer to Leisha the last few years leading up to her death. I still remember when Cait and Breeze weren't able to come to a family reunion one summer and only Leisha and Kathy came. Leisha and I spent the entire time together; heart-to-heart conversations on the school playground, roaming the streets of Lipscomb at night trying not to freak each other out, sneaking Phil and Chelsi into the school to scare the other girls and buying rings at the Drug Store in Follett. And then later we had the family reunion in Kansas and none of the other cousins came to that, so it was just us. It was a blast! I remember that summer being the turning point in our relationship--we never ran out of things to talk about and she never failed to make me laugh.

Michael W. Smith's "I Hear Leesha" really helped me during the months following her death. It is eerie how fitting that song turned out to be. Before she died, I thought of her whenever I heard of it simply due to the name, but now it's impossible not to connect to the song lyrically. The line "Oh, I hear Leisha, telling me that she's alright" really helped me deal with the loss. Because where she is now--she's perfect.

Kelsey Honigford Adams

Leisha was sunshine, optimism and hope. When she smiled, her eyes lit up. When you lose someone like that, it changes you if you even knew her a little and I knew her a lot. I knew her past the smiles to the insecurities. I knew her past the sunshine to the darker storms. I knew the fight she put up to stay hopeful. And when you lose your best friend and stronghold, you're bound to change.

For me, thankfully, the change was good. Instead of becoming bitter and hard, I became more like her. I strove to find the good in situations. I saw the ugly but chose to focus on the good. When Leisha met me, I was on the path to chaos. When she left me, she left me in a better place. Because of her love for God and her determination to challenge me on becoming a better person, I raised my standards for life.

Joanna Suter Rimmer

I grew up going to church with Leisha and working on the (Suter) farm with her. She was such a blast to have at work, making the 5am start time more bearable with her smiling face and big hugs. We never did get to work a stand together but talked about it constantly and how fun that would be! We enjoyed singing songs while picking strawberries and making up new games while sacking corn. We also went on several missions trips together and enjoyed growing closer to the Lord. She was such a great encourager to me, asking me how my walk with the Lord was and steering me in the right direction when I wanted to go my own way. I'm so thankful for her love of others and teaching me to not judge people around me.

A few months after Leisha's death, my cousin passed away. I

remember asking God why he was taking these people from me and causing me and my family and friends so much pain. I remember being in so much pain that I would go outside and cut my arms with pieces of broken glass just to feel a different pain. After several weeks of this, God had enough. I was out under the stars and heard him speak to me, asking me why I was causing him so much pain by hurting myself. My eyes were opened at that point and I saw the pain I was causing God. He reminded me of the pain he felt when Christ died on the cross and how much pain He felt when Leisha died. He reminded me that he is in control and knows what he's doing, even when it doesn't make sense to us. I felt so much hope and love that night and a little understanding.

If I could say one thing to Leisha today, I would say Thank you! You were and still are an image bearer of Christ. You pointed people to him, not yourself. You loved unconditionally and taught others how to do the same. You were a true friend and sister in Christ.

Elizabeth Bell Richards

Excerpts from an English Essay in Feb 2009:

Leisha was one of those girls that everyone adored. At the age of only fifteen, her blonde curly hair and blue eyes caught everyone's attention, along with her bubbly personality. She was a typical social butterfly. The sound of her sparkling laugh or a simple hello from her would brighten anyone's day. However the greatest thing about her, and the thing that I envied the most, was the bold faith and love that she had for God.

...When we reached the accident site I remember dozens of cars lined the sides of the road. The number of mourners present to comfort her family and friends was astounding....My mind drifted back to a few weeks prior to the accident. Leisha and I had volunteered to help lead a junior high overnight retreat. After a powerful worship service we all broke into groups of three junior high students and two high school leaders. Dana, a small timid seventh grader, broke down and began to sob. With a soothing voice Leisha spoke words of reassurance from familiar Bible passages. Dana then decided to dedicate her life to Christ. I sat there in awe of Leisha's confidence. Jealousy overcame me, after all she was a year younger than me and was so comfortable with sharing the gospel with people.

Suddenly I felt someone put their arm around me, causing me to return to reality. It was Leisha's mom. To this day I will never forget what she told us. "You girls have to finish what she started." We looked at each other, knowing that we had a mission to complete. We were responsible for spreading the love of Jesus to anyone and everyone, the way Leisha did.

I have come to see her death as an inspiring event. After all, her passing transformed me into a bolder Christian. I no longer care what people think of me when I stand up for my beliefs. She has given me the hope and desire to impact the lives of those around me, the way she did mine, by spreading the love that Jesus Christ has for each and every person in the world.

Jameson Ridge

Losing a friend at a young age taught me to ensure that those around you know how much you care for them; they could be taken in an instant. Moreover, I learned that my time on earth to make a difference and to leave a legacy is both short and unpredictable. Leisha lived every day seeking and living out the purpose that God created for her life. I believe that after Leisha died, I became more intentional about finding my God-given purpose and living to show love to others. I experienced a desire to be more open with other people, step outside my comfort zone, and expand my sphere of influence.

This experience taught me how to cope at a young age. Emotions such as stress and grief can be very hard to deal with, especially as an adolescent. While losing Leisha taught me how to rely on God's strength and comfort, it also helped me learn other ways to deal with sadness and frustration. For me these include running and exercise, writing or journaling my experiences, and finding someone (or a few people) whom you trust that you can share what you are feeling or experiencing.

I now have a job which in part involves caring for children and adolescents who lack coping mechanisms or an effective support system. I pray that God can use what He taught me through Leisha's death to be able to identify and help young people who are going through difficult circumstances.

I would describe Leisha as fearless and authentic. She met any challenge head-on exuding great confidence, but never once pretended to be perfect. She was outgoing and fun-loving. Her ability to be genuine allowed her to become friends with everyone. In the midst of struggles, I remember Leisha being ever hopeful of God's faithfulness, even when a situation was difficult or didn't make sense. While that doesn't mean she never acknowledged frustration in certain circumstances, she continually viewed trials as an opportunity to rely on God and pursue him.

If I could say something to her, I would thank her for always being true to herself. I would tell her that even though we were the same age and practically friends since birth, I always looked up to her as a role model. I would want her to know how much her friendship meant to me, and how her life had so much more of an impact than she knew.

Jared Millisor

I think in dealing with the grief, I learned that there are some horrible things that occur in life; irrevocable or unfixable events that you just have to accept. And while you shouldn't live in fear of them, you should understand they could happen at any time and you should be upfront with the things you can do today.

If I could speak with her again for just a day, I'd say thank you. The day before she died I had contemplated calling her and thanking her for everything she had done in my life. Her friendship, her kindness, and her stubbornness that changed me in ways I still don't fully comprehend. I decided not to make that call because we were supposed to go to her house that Friday and all have dinner together. I was convinced in person would be better and I'd do it then. I never got that Friday or made that call which saddens me, but I am thankful for every day I got to have her in my life. So if I got that chance I'd tell her how much she has meant to me. She was one of the most wonderful, beautiful, and magnificent individuals I have ever met in my life.

Jason Suter

Excerpt from class paper Sept 2007 called *Live Life to the Full.*

Leisha Burrus, a fifteen year old bubbly young lady, had a goal for her life. She wanted to impact people. She wanted, above all, to lean people towards her friend and Savior, Jesus Christ. She was on fire for God. Every chance she got a hold of she would tell someone about God. She would tell of his amazing love, mercy, and forgiveness. She would tell, most of all, about God's wonderful, beautiful, perfect Son, Jesus. Every night she would pray that God would use her for something amazing. Leisha wanted to impact the entire world.

God did answer Leisha's prayers, in a way that nobody would have ever imagined. Leisha's death impacted more people than anyone could ever track down. The next day, at the produce farm where she and her two sisters worked, there was a short prayer service held for her. A young man prayed and everyone cried. Seeds were planted in the hearts of many of the workers who did not know Jesus the way Leisha did. Those present who knew Jesus were also touched. None of their lives would ever be the same. A piece, a chunk, a part of everyone's life was ripped away.

Leisha lived a full life in Christ Jesus. She didn't live to a ripe old age physically, but she did live long and fruitful spiritually. Leisha is an excellent example of someone who grabbed life and ran with it. She lived like every day was her last. The easiest thing to be learned from Leisha is that no one knows how long he or she has on this earth, and everyone should live accordingly. The most important thing Leisha would want everyone to learn is that Jesus' love covers all. Jesus forgives any and all sin. He died as a sacrifice for the world's sin. Jesus is the way, the truth, and the life (John 14:6). Jesus died so that you might have life and have it to the full (John 10:10). Leisha believed this with all her heart, soul, and mind. Her prayer is that you would as well.

Tabby Lewis

Our relationship was cut short, but just in that short time I was starting to think of Leisha as an older sister figure. I looked up to Leisha. She seemed so mature and carried a lot of wisdom for just being two years older than me. I admired that. She was someone that I could trust with my thoughts and struggles in my teenage life.

There have been many times when I needed to think of Leisha and this idea of trying to have hope in this brown world. I really needed to have hope when I was a freshman in college and got a call that my dad had a seizure and was on a breathing machine. My heart sank when I first heard because I thought the worst. I am going to lose my dad, my best friend. I turn to him for everything in my life. I was scared that I wasn't going to see him again. Rushing home, I thought of Romans 15:13 and John 14:27. God was giving me peace and hope. After thinking about those verses and thinking about the things I learned from Leisha I knew my dad was going to pull through and sure enough he did. If I hadn't met Leisha I don't think I would have been hopeful and looked to Christ.

Tabby was in the Jr Hi group that Leisha led as a Sr. Hi student leader at our church. I, Kathy, spoke of her earlier in the book as well. The spring before this book was published, Tabby graduated as an art major from Huntington University. Rennie and I attended her Senior Art Exhibit and were captivated by her display entitled
Hope in a Hurticane.

Tabby's description of her art speaks clearly of this exhibit:

...I created the series of urns to symbolize the three individuals who had a great impact on my life. The last urn is dedicated to my friend Leisha who had taught me many lessons that I still carry with me today. God brought her into my life just when I needed her. I only got to share about a year with Leisha until she wasn't there anymore. She left a huge impact on my life in the short time I got to spend with her. I struggled a while with the fact that I didn't attend her funeral even though she meant a lot to me. Soon after I decided that I wasn't going to live my life in sadness and depression. Leisha wouldn't have done that. She taught me that even though we live in a messy, dirty world, Christ can come into our lives and bring us hope.

Kayleen Meckle, cousin

Even though Leisha and I were cousins, distance prevented us from being as close as we could have been. I was 17 when Leisha died and I still remember exactly where I was, who I was with, and the immediate shock and disbelief I felt. This was the first death in my life involving someone in my family who was so young. One thing I learned was that we are not invincible when we are young even though we think we are untouchable. The sanctity of life has been impressed on me even more strongly because of Leisha's death. It could happen at any moment, to anyone. I have been through several more deaths of friends and family since 2006 and I still don't know if I have mastered the art of dealing with grief. I tend to withdraw, shut down and not let anyone in to help me. However, going through a death of someone so young has enabled me to understand the grieving process more fully, especially regarding the families involved.

The main thing I will remember from Leisha's funeral was the number of people who attended, the lives she touched while she was alive and the celebrative atmosphere of the whole ordeal. She was full of joy in life and death. I can't wait to see her again!

Kara Piatt, cousin

I was 15 when Leisha died. The thing I struggled with the most was, *why her?* Why of all the people God could take home, would she be the one? Leisha was one of those people you just wanted to be around. She had a smile and outlook that was infectious. I couldn't understand why her, because I thought God could do so much through her and she could touch so many lives, that there is no reason that she should have died.

I never would have said that I was questioning God, because I knew in my head that you weren't supposed to question God. But truth be told, I was. I don't know how long it took me to stop questioning, but I decided that maybe God would use her death to draw more people to him than her life would have. I won't ever be able to say if that's true or not, but I believe that God has it under control, and I have to trust him, even if I don't get the answers.

God used Leisha's death to draw me closer to him. When you are down and don't know where to turn, God is there. At the age of 15, and dealing with the death of a loved one who was also 15, it was hard for me to deal with death. But now, so many years later, one thing that I have taken away from her death is that I need to make the most of every opportunity. You never know how much time you have here on earth, so when you get the feeling you need to talk with someone, take it. You never know what God can use you for if you don't step out in faith.

Leisha made such an impact on my life, and probably never realized it. She may not have been doing it on purpose but every time we got together she made me feel special. Even though we were the same age, I looked up to her. God used her, during her life and through her death, to touch my life. I miss her greatly, I can find comfort because I know she is with Jesus in a much better place.

Jane Munk, Leisha's counselor

Letter to Leisha: 8-20-2006
Today, the day of your funeral, I got to know you best. Somehow I also felt that this was your destiny. To die at 15 years old hardly seems long enough in the traditional way we think of life. Something today gave me peace, not only that you are home in heaven, but that this is your calling, your legacy.

The world will remember you always as the 15 year old. You will never grow old. Your spirit will remain as the vivacious young woman who brought light. You are teaching me in your death. Yes, a 41 year old woman. Yet I really think that your intent was to just live your life as the girl you were. You did not intend to "teach" this middle aged person, or maybe anyone. You just lived fully as you understood what that was.

I wondered today, why it is so easy for me to accept your short life, when I struggle to understand other lives that seemingly ended too soon. God is teaching me, I am not sure what, but your life is being used in mine.

As I looked around at the many people who came to express their love, I was reminded of the impact one life can really have. Many in the room were holding their loved ones just a little bit closer. Most shed tears and felt deeply. Some were trying to look like they were not so deeply moved, but we all were.

You will be missed, yet you will live on. Thank you for touching my life. I love you.

(Jane has since founded Kerith Brook Retreats for Grieving Adults. For more information, go to kerithbrook.org.)

About the Author

Kathy Burrus serves several roles in life. She is a wife, mother, a daughter herself and friend. She is a leader of worship that lifts the chins of people to see the face of God. She is a lover of stories, and more importantly, of the people who live those stories. That is what drew her to be a life coach; to help people intentionally design hope in their life, love and loss.

Drawing from her experience as a life coach and former pastor's wife, Kathy shares a message of hope and healing to women that is authentically transparent.

Kathy and her husband, Rennie, have been married for 37 years. They are the parents of three beautiful daughters; Caitlin, Brielle, and Leisha, and now enjoy the presence of two sons-in-law; Jack and Jason. Kathy and Rennie live in Columbus Grove, Ohio.

Kathy received a Bachelor of Science degree from Grace College of the Bible (now Grace University) of Omaha, NE with a double major in Bible and Church Music in 1980. She became a Certified Professional Coach *(MCC, CPC, CLC, CRC, CBEC)* in the areas of Life, Relationship and Bereavement in 2011 from *World Coach Institute (WCI),* an *International Coaching Federation (ICF)* approved school and is now an instructor for WCI.

Kathy enjoys hosting tea parties with her grandmother's china, listening to music that matches her mood, and observing nature in some of her favorite spaces. Add to that some precious time with family and friends and she is one happy lady.

To schedule Kathy for your women's event or conference,
or to learn more about her ministry
and how she can help you listen to your story,
visit www.kathyburrus.com.

Acknowledgements

To each of you I mention here and many others along the way, you are super heroes in my life. To have your support and the influence of your story in this work is truly a gift. Thank you.

Pat, Christy and Barbara: You have each shown up in my life with your unique contribution at just the right times. Thank you for giving me eyes to see, courage to continue and support when I feared the next step. Your prayers, encouragement and challenge have been invaluable to this process of writing, but more importantly, to my journey to this place.

First Look Readers: Barbara Hubbell, Pat Emery Hixon, Christy Dean, Janice Rayl, Lydia Tschetter, Cyndy Bergmaier, Kristen Bergmaier, Pam Eubanks, and Judy Schultz. Thank you for daring to read the early drafts and then some. Each one of your insights has spoken to a particular enhancement to this project.

Eileen Hartles, Jenny Thiessen, Calli Stephens: Thank you for taking my 'mess' of words and helping me to clean them up to be better understood. I am so grateful for your specific attention to detail.

Teresa Boyer: I am so grateful that you were recommended to me as an editor over and over again. Thank you for helping me own my voice and the message that I need to speak.

Lovely Traces Launch Team
Thank you seems so trite for how I feel toward you. But I do thank you for your interest in and support of the book and my journey, not just in writing it, but in getting to the point that I could write. Some of you have walked the journey for a while now. Your notes and emails of encouragement have been timely and life-giving. Thank you for sharing this work with your world. I am eternally grateful for your prayers during the writing and even now as it goes out to leave its *lovely traces of hope* on those who read it.

Hannah Nitz, Kory and Cheri Hubbell, Stan Long: Each of you stepped in at just the right moment to help me SEE and SAY what I needed to see and say. I so love having you in my journey.

JoAnn Fore, Abby Alleman, and the Free Your Story Group: Thank you for encouraging me to use my voice even if others were saying something similar to my message.

Christine Niles at writersnextstep.com. Thanks for believing in me before you even knew me. Your coaching was timely and desperately needed.

Jeff Goins and the Tribewriter Community: You inspired me to set the date for this book to be published, not to mention supplied me with some incredible tools to work through the process of writing and launching.

Jennifer Wenzke and the So Now Network of Women: Your gift of encouragement and support has spurred me on more than I can say. Thank you for reminding me of my own worth and the value I bring to others.

Becky Harling and the Creative Communication Mastermind: You helped me clarify my message and see the person I was writing it for. Becky, your mentoring and your books have been such a gift in my life. Thanks for being ahead of me in the journey so you can help point the way.

Linda Dillow: You have been a precious example in life, marriage, and worship most of my adult life though we have only met a dozen times or so. I am so grateful that someone gave me your first book for a wedding gift. I'm grateful that the Lord intersected our stories, from Texas to Colorado, Ukraine to Ohio. Just when I needed to take a next step, you put out your next book.

You have led me in a journey of contentment, worship, marriage, and sex even. You encouraged me to find peace in my life and to see my words, attitudes, work, my waiting—and even my pain—as an act of worship. You led me in worship, not in songs of worship, but in worship of two hearts bowed at the sofa, remembering who God is, recalling what he has done and praising him from the core of our beings.

I am humbled and grateful that you have written this foreword for the book.

Notes

Introduction
        1.   Revelation 1: 17-19 NLT

Chapter 1
        1.   Leisha's Journal

Chapter 2
        1.   Thiessen, Lovella, **Leisha's genealogy**, Used by permission.
        2.   Psalm 44:1   KJV
        3.   Psalm 78:4   KJV
        4.   Tolkien, J.R., **Lord of the Rings, The Two Towers #2**, quoted by John Eldredge in **EPIC: The Story God is Telling and the Role that is Yours to Play,** (Thomas Nelson, Nashville, TN 2004) 1

Chapter 4
        1.   Burrus, Kathy, **What's Your Story telling You?** (Life Map, www.kathyburrus.com) 31
        2.   **Life Story-Community: Discovering Who We Are Together**, (Dallas Theological Seminar, Dallas, Texas, Center for Christian Leadership)
        3.   Allender, Dan, **To Be Told: God Invites You to Coauthor Your Future** (Colorado Springs, CO: WaterBrook Press, 2005), 10.
        4.   Soren Kierkegaard, apparent resource is **Søren Kierkegaards Skrifter,** (Søren Kierkegaard Research Center, Copenhagen, 1997--) volume 18, 306.
                   å

Chapter 5
        1.   Allender, Dan, **To Be Told: God Invites You to Coauthor Your Future** (Colorado Springs, CO: WaterBrook Press, 2005), 1
        2.   Tina English, **Even Before You Were Born** (song), © 1980 Word Music, LLC (a div. of Word Music Group, Inc.) All rights reserved. Used with permission.

Chapter 6

1. Allender, Dan, **To Be Told: God Invites You to Coauthor Your Future** (Colorado Springs, CO: WaterBrook Press, 2005), 29
2. Michael W. Smith, Andy Stanley, and Robert Sterling, **The Big Picture** musical, (Word Music, 1991)
3. Michael W. Smith and Wayne Kirkpatrick, **I Hear Leesha**, © 1988 Universal Music - Brentwood Benson Songs (Admin. by Brentwood-Benson Music Publishing, Inc.) Sony/ATV Milene Music (Admin. by Sony/ATV Music Publishing) Used with permission.
4. L.M. Montgomery, **Anne of Avonlea, (Anne of Green Gables**, #2, 1909)
5. Romans 12:3-6   NIV
6. Stephens, Andrea, **Girlfriend, You Are a B.A.B.E,** (Baker Publishing Group, 2005)) Used with permission of author, B.A.B. E. description was also published in Brio Magazine, a magazine for young girls by Focus on the Family magazine which has since been discontinued.

Chapter 7

1. Burrus, Caitlin R, **WORDS,** Used by permission.

Chapter 8

1. Sittser, Jerry, **A Grace Disguised: How the Soul Grows Through Loss**, (Zondervan, Grand Rapids, MI 1995, 2004) www.zondervan.com, 9
2. Sittser, Jerry, **A Grace Disguised: How the Soul Grows Through Loss**, (Zondervan, Grand Rapids, MI 1995, 2004) www.zondervan.com, 9

Chapter 9

1. Wilkinson, Bruce, **The Dream Giver,** (Multnomah Publishers, Inc., Sisters, OR 2003) 45
2. Wilkinson, Bruce, **The Dream Giver,** (Multnomah Publishers, Inc., Sisters, OR 2003), 47
3. Moore, Steve and David T. Clydesdale, **Evidence of Grace, A Worship Musical Tracing God's Hand of Mercy,** © 2002 Word Music, a division of Word Music Group, LLC.
4. Craig, Shawn and Connie Harrington, **Your Grace Still Amazes Me,** (© 2001 Ariose Music and Praise Song Press (admin. By EMI Christian Music Publication). Used with Permission.

Chapter 10

1. Sittser, Jerry, **A Grace Disguised: How the Soul Grows Through Loss**, (Zondervan, Grand Rapids, MI 1995, 2004) www.zondervan.com, 9

2. Sittser, Jerry, **A Grace Disguised: How the Soul Grows Through Loss**, (Zondervan, Grand Rapids, MI 1995, 2004) www.zondervan.com, 9

3. Allender, Dan, **To Be Told: God Invites You to Coauthor Your Future** (Colorado Springs, CO: WaterBrook Press, 2005), 34

Chapter 11

1. Michael W. Smith and Wayne Kirkpatrick, **I Hear Leesha**, © 1988 Universal Music - Brentwood Benson Songs (Admin. by Brentwood-Benson Music Publishing, Inc.) Sony/ATV Milene Music (Admin. by Sony/ATV Music Publishing) Used with permission.

Chapter 12

1. Nimmo, Beth, **The Journal of Rachel Scott, a Real Diary of Faith**, (©2001, published by Tommy Nelson, a division of Thomas Nelson, Inc., Nashville, TN)

2. Revelation 1:10-19   NLT

3. Baloche, Paul, **All the Earth Will Sing Your Praises**, © 2003 Integrity's Hosanna! Music (ASCAP) (admin. at CapitolCMGPublishing.com) All rights reserved. Used by permission.

4. Eaton, Chris, **My Father's Heart**, performed by Rachel Lampa, © 2000 SGO Music Publishing Ltd. (Admin. by Dayspring Music, LLC) All rights reserved. Used with permission.

5. Psalm 28:7   NIV

6. Meyers, Krystal and Ian Ashley Eskeline, **Lovely Traces**, Copyright © 2005 Bridge Building Music (BMI) Designer Music (SESAC) Koobie Tunes (SESAC) Starshaped Music (BMI) (admin. At CapitolCMGPublishing.com)
Special Provisions: Title use also permitted for this project. All rights reserved. Used by permission.

Part 5: Green Means Hope

1. Artwork by Brielle Burrus Augsburger, **110 Days of Green**, 2008, Used with permission.

Chapter 13

1. Brown, Brene, **Rising Strong: The Reckoning, the Rumble, the Revolution,** (© 2015 by Brene Brown, Spiegel and Grau, an imprint of Random House, a division of Penguin Random House, LLC, New York), Introduction xxiv.

2. Brown, Brene, **Rising Strong: The Reckoning, the Rumble, the Revolution,** (© 2015 by Brene Brown, Spiegel and Grau, an imprint of Random House, a division of Penguin Random House, LLC, New York), Introduction xxiv

Chapter 14

1. Sittser, Jerry, **A Grace Disguised: How the Soul Grows Through Loss**, (Zondervan, Grand Rapids, MI 1995, 2004) www.zondervan.com, 33
2. Sittser, Jerry, **A Grace Disguised: How the Soul Grows Through Loss**, (Zondervan, Grand Rapids, MI 1995, 2004) www.zondervan.com, 33-34
3. Revelation 1:17-19   NLT
4. Revelation 4:6-8   NLT
5. Sittser, Jerry, **A Grace Disguised: How the Soul Grows Through Loss**, (Zondervan, Grand Rapids, MI 1995, 2004) www.zondervan.com, 35
6. Sittser, Jerry, **A Grace Disguised: How the Soul Grows Through Loss**, (Zondervan, Grand Rapids, MI 1995, 2004) www.zondervan.com, 36

Chapter 15

1. Exodus 13: 17-18 NIV
2. Exodus 14: 21-22 NIV
3. Exodus 15:1-2   NIV
4. Deuteronomy 31:6   NIV
5. Joshua 1:5   NIV

Chapter 16

1. Exodus 14:13-14   NIV
2. Mark 1:15   NIV
3. John 3:16   KJV

Chapter 17

1. Kubler-Ross, Elizabeth, and David Kessler, **On Grief and Grieving** (Scribner, A Division of Simon and Schuster, Inc., New York, NY, 2005)
2. Jeremiah 29:11 NIV
3. Mark 1:15   NIV
4. Mark 1:15   Amplified
5. Pritchard, Dr. Ray, regarding Charles Blondin, internet article, http://www.crosswalk.com/blogs/dr-ray-pritchard/the-great-blondin-and-true-saving-faith

Chapter 18

1. Hinkle, Jason, **Wind of God,** lyrics used with permission.
2. John 11:25   NLT
3. Luke 10: 41-42 NIV
4. John 11: 5   NLT
5. John 11:20-21   NLT

6. John 11:22-24 NLT
7. John 11:25-26   NLT
8. John 11: 27   NLT
9. John 11:32   NLT
10. Harling, Becky, **Finding Calm in Life's Chaos,** (NavPress, Colorado Spring, CO 2005) 98
11. Isaiah 43:1-5   NLT
12. John 11:33-37   NLT
13. Burge, Gary M., **John 11:34, The NIV Application Commentary: John** (Zondervan, Grand Rapids, Michigan 2000) 318
14. John 11:35   NLT
15. Harling, Becky, **Finding Calm in Life's Chaos,** (NavPress, Colorado Spring, CO 2005) 99-100
16. John 11: 38-42 NLT
17. Harling, Becky, **Finding Calm in Life's Chaos,** (NavPress, Colorado Spring, CO 2005) 101

Chapter 19

1. Nouwen, Henry, **With Open Hands,** (Ave Maria Press, Inc., 1972, 1995, 2005) 20
2. Dillow, Linda, **Calm My Anxious Heart: A Woman's Guide to Finding Contentment,** (NavPress, Colorado Spring, CO 1998) 179-184.
3. Habakkuk 3:1-2   NLT
4. Habakkuk 3: 16-19   NLT

Journal Entry: April 28, 2013

1. Millard, Bart, Performed by Mercy Me, **I Can Only Imagine,** © 2001 Simpleville Music ASCAP (admin. By Simpleville Publishing, LLC c/o Music Services, Inc.) International copyright secured. All rights reserves. Used by permission.
2. Breck, Carrie Elizabeth Ellis and Grant Colfax Tullar, **Face to Face I shall Behold Him,** © Words: Public Domain

Chapter 20

1. Romans 8:28   NLT
2. Jeremiah 29:11   NLT
3. Psalm 51:6   NLT
4. Psalm 77:1-6,   NLT
5. Psalm 77: 7-10   NLT
6. Sittser, Jerry, **When God Doesn't Answer Your Prayer: Insights to Keep You praying with Greater Faith and Deeper Hope,** (© 2003, 2007 by Gerald L. Sittser Zondervan, Grand Rapids, MI), 65.
7. Sittser, Jerry, **When God Doesn't Answer Your Prayer: Insights to Keep You praying with Greater Faith and Deeper Hope,** (© 2003, 2007 by Gerald L. Sittser Zondervan, Grand Rapids, MI), 66

8. Psalm 77:11-12   NLT
9. Dillow, Linda, **The Blessing Book**, (© 2003, NavPress, Colorado Springs, CO) 32
10. Psalm 77: 13-20   NLT
11. Nouwen, Henry, **With Open Hands,** (Ave Maria Press, Inc., 1972, 1995, 2005) 72, quote from one of Nouwen's students.

Journal Entry: January 30, 2016
1. 2 Corinthians 4:6-10 NLT

Chapter 21
1. Ingram, Chip, **Holy Ambition: What it Takes to Make a Difference for God** (Moody Press, Chicago, IL 2002) 93
2. Hebrews 11:1, 6   NLT
3. Revelation 1:18   NLT
4. John 11:35   NLT
5. Romans 15:13   MSG
6. Nordeman, Nichole, **Legacy,** (© 2002 Ariose Music) (Admin. by Capitol CMG Publishing) Used with permission.

Tracing Your Story
1. Buechner, Frederick, **Now and Then: A Memoir of Vocation** (HarperCollins Publishers, New York, NY 1983)

Epilogue
1. Artwork by Brielle Burrus, **Once Upon A Summertime,** 2006, Used with permission.